Power

and

Put-on

BY JOSEPH S. LOBENTHAL, JR.

Growing Up Clean In America

Power
and
Put-on

THE LAW

IN

AMERICA

JOSEPH S. LOBENTHAL, JR.

OUTERBRIDGE & DIENSTFREY · NEW YORK

DISTRIBUTED BY E. P. DUTTON & CO.

Library of Congress number 72-126583
First published in
the United States of America in 1970
Copyright © 1970 by Outerbridge & Dienstfrey.

Design: Victoria Dudley

Outerbridge & Dienstfrey

200 West 72 Street, New York 10023

To
Shirley
and Joel and Nicky and Lyd
for many missed private days and nights
and
to the family of Tony—
a boy from the Soul and Latin Theater of
East Harlem,
who died on April 25, 1970,
from a bad nickel-bag or an overdose,
at nineteen.

ACKNOWLEDGMENTS

For convenience, everything is described in the first person. All the names, of course, are fictitious and the cases I discuss are disguised. Originally, I had intended to write, for safety's sake, that all the cases and specific examples were fictitious. But this would have been a fiction itself. The fact is that, so far as I know, they are all true.

Most of what is described here I participated in or observed. A few episodes were reliably reported in courtroom corridors or by other lawyers in those ordinary conversations, over drinks or lunch, that often take place among people in the same business who are sharing, looking for solace or advice, or just unwinding. Some illustrations are composites from my ten years in general practice—first as a law associate, then as a sole practitioner, and, most recently, as a partner in a two-man firm.

My greatest debt of gratitude, therefore, must be to those members of the bar who unwittingly became subjects, of a sort, for this self-study of an occupation and a system. (Notwithstanding the fact that I already have had indications that the book is going to prove violently unwelcome in some of the same quarters that served as my sources, I believe that, on the whole, it will receive fair treatment within the profession.) More immediately, I am indebted to a very small group of lawyers, preferring to remain anonymous, who were willing to climb down from their professional hobbyhorses and take time out to enter into serious discussions about the nature and meaning of their life's work.

The experiences taken from, so to speak, outlying parts of the legal system are also ones that I have personally garnered over the years. For a time, I worked in the New York City prison system. Later I served as a consultant to other correctional, probation, parole, and antidelinquency groups, and I was the director and general counsel of a federally sponsored research project, mentioned later, that studied the effectiveness of various correctional techniques. Many colleagues from these groups and associates in these endeavors informally shared with me their workaday thoughts and, therefore, although they cannot be named, must be acknowledged as the real source for much of my material.

The Frederick A. Moran Memorial Institute on Crime and Delinquency meets for one week each year on the campus of St. Lawrence University, New York. Students in my classes and workshops there are professional workers in rehabilitation, enforcement, and correction. It is a pleasure to acknowledge how much I learned from them about the other side of the coin—insights that could never have been gained with just the perspective of a practicing lawyer.

The Yale dissertation I quote at some length in Part I is Douglas Rosenthal's "Client Participation in Professional

Decisions: the Lawyer-Client Relationship in Personal Injury Cases" (1970, unpublished). I have had some fun with this work in order to make a point, but in several interviews with the author I always found him to be a sensitive and knowledgeable individual. These discussions provided me with a further impetus for wanting to "set the record straight" with respect to what I believe really takes place in the legal maze. I consider his thesis essentially accurate despite our different viewpoints.

For a number of years I have been teaching about the politics of law. Many ideas in this book were developed during stimulating exchanges with serious and thoughtful students from all walks of life who were interested enough to take these courses. I am greatly indebted to them, naturally, but also to Allen Austill, dean of the New School for Social Research, who was always not only receptive to new ideas for inclusion in his catalogue, but downright excited by them. I know of no educator whose concept of what an urban university should be in these turbulent times makes more sense. He has patience for the untried and the experimental, and at the same time, being the old humanist that he is, Dean Austill's concern for the best of the past reciprocally fires-up the innovators—which is very much responsible for making the school the good place to work and learn that it is.

Two other persons in particular should be signaled out. This is not to pin them with the rap of any specific contribution to the following pages but to say that over the years, they consistently have stimulated new ideas and have been patient with the variety of formulations about the legal system and its adjuncts that I brought to them. Neither is a lawyer; both are friends with whom I have been associated in a number of law-related endeavors. Milton Luger is a public administrator, Douglas Gosnell a sociologist—yet each is considerably more. Each must be cited for his remarkable clarity (though each demonstrates it his own way), that ability to get directly to the heart of a matter and to look at an activity or an essay critically, objectively and, still, with sympathy. When discussing ideas that have found their way into this book, they were of tremendous value as creative touchstones. They generously and frequently offered welcome intellectual comfort to an occupational schizophrenic—being, themselves, probably the same.

My friend, Theodore Thomte, made a thorough and painstakingly critical review of a draft of this entire manuscript. He offered the incalculable benefit of his shrewd, insightful, and wide-ranging thinking and also his experience as a man of many interests that are relevant to the topic.

After all is said and done, it would be ingratitude not to mention a considerable debt to Harris Dienstfrey, my more-than-editor, to whom I am thankful for the precise combination of cajolery, coercion, cavilling and cradling that was instrumental in getting this book out on time and in its present form.

Contents

OLD SCHOOL TIES

THE ECONOMICS OF CONSCIENCE

PERSPECTIVES, PERCEPTIONS, AND REFLECTIONS

II IN THE MAZE

INTRODUCTION

You walk into a lawyer's office with a problem and some notion of what you want. You come out with a bill—and never really find out what it means or what your money bought.

In a rare case, you may ask for clarification of the bill's phrase, "for professional services rendered." When you do, you may be treated to another level of jargon: "investigation," "conferences," "research," "attendance in court," and "negotiations"—words that are supposed to put your doubts to rest.

But clients for the most part have long been satisfied to keep their respectful distance. This enables legal professionals and insiders to free wheel in a world that, as we shall see, spins unto itself, for them alone. But if their private planet didn't also somehow serve—or seem to serve—the needs of others, it wouldn't spin for long.

Two approaches—both incomplete—are commonly accepted as adequate for comprehending what the law is all about. The first involves studying the decisions of famous judges and resembles a catechism on the Thoughts of Chairman So-and-So. The second involves analyzing the exploits of heroes of the practicing bar and exposing the misdeeds of its villains.

Neither approach is capable of offering serious enlightenment about the legal system. One is an intellectual exercise, perpetuating the fiction that law adapts to changing social conditions through a timeless set of self-contained rules of logic and fairness. The other, personalizing the law, is an entertainment, sheer sport. Central as the lawyer's role is, he serves mainly as an expediter. He is an aid, guiding clients through the maze of the legal system—while at the same time he helps to keep that system intact. Moreover, how he goes about his work is, among other things, a reflection of those who find it useful or necessary to hire him.

While the law *is* both a mental exercise and an amusement, it is also considerably more, something that I try to indicate in the following pages.

By simultaneously presenting front-stage and back-stage views of the action (to borrow a concept from Erving Goffman), I try to show not only the lawyer's work but also several of the forces that make him—and the law as such—work. I draw on examples from several agencies and activities within the legal system, not only just those involving lawyers. Taken together, they provide a picture of the legal system in action.

I consider, in the first part of the book, typical participants within this system—clients, lawyers, policemen, judges—and their relationships with each other at strategic points of interaction. The second part is concerned with representative bureaucracies in the legal structure. Both parts attempt to illustrate how the individual is related to the bureaucracy and how the activities of each—individual and bureaucracy—are interlocked with hidden forces and interests-at-large but are not commonly believed to play an official part, much less a critical role, in the formal legal apparatus.

I have not rushed to impose my own interpretations on the episodes presented here. It is precisely my thesis that the average client (or potential client) should be wary of official doctrine promulgated by professionals. He ought to question the pronouncements of all the professions that are allied within the law bureaucracy. This requires some degree of discomfort because legal professionalism offers the lay citizen an image of itself that essentially absolves him of responsibility for what takes place behind the scenes. In any case, I have let the illustrations speak for themselves with the hope that the reader will feel compelled to become involved—as his own advocate.

A last point. It may be argued that this is a book about law in New York City or, at most, any large American city— not necessarily about law across the nation. I would contend that the general outlines of practice are the same all over. Only the props of the law's magic-show vary, depending on the setting, the competition around town, the particular needs and demands of local customers, and the prices that customers can afford or are willing to pay. While the illustrations on which I rely are drawn from the kinds of cases with which I have greatest familiarity and are selected because they are likely to have been encountered by a reader, the themes they are intended to point up apply equally, from what I have observed, to all levels of practice—ranging from massive and powerful Wall Street firms to one-man neighborhood practices with offices in storefronts, from corporate house-counsel to civil rights agency staff lawyers.

In all instances, as with hi-fi components, the initial choice is with the customer. To an extent, of course, his expectations are manufactured by advertisements. And he is limited by what is available on the market. But, although he may be unaware of the electronics involved, the sound that finally comes out of the speakers—after amplification and removal of "distortions"—is engineered to his taste. The law's components operate similarly. They are marketed, at a profit, to please the customer. The sounds that come from the speakers must satisfy.

I

THE GUIDES
AND THE MAZE

"It's the union that makes
people professionals."
—Albert Shanker, President,
United Federation of Teachers, June 3, 1970

1

LAWYER
BUSINESS

In one law school final at the University of Chicago, just getting through a reading of the questions seemed beyond me. Looking around and seeing my classmates transformed in various stages of assured response, I desperately cast myself into a kind of trance and concentrated on the teaching style of the famous professor who had made up this exam. His lectures, if they could be called that, were a series of brittle idea-bursts, unfinished sentences, key phrases, and obscure and mystifying queries that always seemed to shoot out from nowhere, have no possible answer or bearing on what I had been making of the previous discussions, and then, as soon as they hit the air, seemed apparently to vanish.

Carefully centering my paper on the desk, I started to imitate his style: using dashes, question marks, and ellipses in profusion and at random. After a few minutes of warming to the task, case names and nicknames, judge's names, legal principles and concepts from god-knows-where in lavish abundance began flowing onto page after page. I paused several times, just long enough to reflect on where to insert the numbers to designate what question I was supposedly answering. These I decided to place so as to make each answer of a different length—in inverse ratio to the size of the question.

It was after experiencing the pleasant surprise of my grade that I first became intrigued with the law's mystique. What puzzled me most was that even the professor, or his graduate assistant in charge of grading the papers, had been taken in, confusing style with content and rewarding bravado as if it were knowledge.

After graduation from law school, I served three years as a Naval officer, considered going back to graduate studies in literature but decided, instead, to take a job in city government and apply for admission to the bar. When I got promoted, I thought seriously, but briefly, about remaining in government. Almost at the same time, however, I received an offer to enter general practice, the kind that supposedly involved people—not just paper. Status, money, the hurly-burly of "real" problems and, perhaps, a peek at power all beckoned. Besides, I expected, I was about to experience the reality behind law school abstractions and to understand the mystique of professionalism.

I started working for two lawyers—in a storefront office on New York's Lower East Side. These two bosses rated the suite's lone private office—taking turns, depending on whose client it was, behind the large mahogany desk there. I occupied a smaller desk in a small working area which was separated by a wooden fence from a still smaller reception

area. This work space I shared with a lame real estate operator and his wife, who assisted him—both professionally and
in ambulation, particularly through the gate in the fence—
and with one secretary whom, in turn, we all shared. Coffee
money was always available from a kitty stocked with fees
for notarial services that we performed for relief recipients,
who brought in their forms from a welfare center down the
block. For cops from the station house across the street we
performed the same services free, trading them off for protection against the perils of alternate-side-of-the-street parking.

A friend from school led a different life. He was employed
by a big downtown firm, with individual offices larger than
our whole suite. The salary his firm offered recent graduates
exceeded my two employers' combined net.

One evening we kept a promise to meet for drinks. But
his day's work wasn't yet finished. He had to return to the
office to complete merger papers for which approval from
Justice and other government departments was being
sought. As he enthusiastically detailed the intricacies of
these departments' requirements, I became increasingly uncomfortable—and thankful that he seemed too wrapped up
in his own labors to be likely to ask about mine. It would
have been humiliating to disclose that the most complicated
matter I had attended all day was a letter to the rent commission asking whether a neighborhood Polish woman was
being overcharged for her apartment. Negotiations between
our client and one of my chiefs over the total fee for this
transaction had ended at $25—provided, of course, no fur-
ther legal work was involved. I knew that an hour of a senior partner's time in my friend's firm could be reflected in
the billing, perhaps somewhat disguised, at between $500
and $10,000—depending on the client and his business.

It took me ten years, in a steadily uplifted practice, to arrive at the conclusion that my friend and I, in our vastly different offices, were both doing similar things that day: steering our clients' financial interests through a labyrinth of administrative regulations that the clients felt unequipped to manage alone. And our bosses were also striving for the same goal: to get top dollar, under the prevailing conditions.

Law practice, whatever the kind of law and the differences between one case and the next, involves the repetition of a certain basic number of similarly patterned activities and the application of one method of thinking—a modified form of logic. All that varies is the "situational" background, a mix of differing official rules, customs, and attitudes, and of the interplay between vested interests (which depend, in turn, on the relative financial power of these interests).

The lawyer's specialty is a misleading way to categorize his practice. The specialty refers only to the particular "situation" he deals with, the way his office is furnished, how he dresses, what fees he charges, and the books that line his wall. Above all, he deals with people—of two sorts.

First, he deals with those who are ensconced in the system itself, the law professionals: judges, clerks, police, and other lawyers—to mention a few. The other group consists of clients, those who come for the specific purpose of getting help in their own dealings with other law professionals. Clients are consumers of the law, the civilians of the legal system.

A lawyer's job is to reconcile the distinct, mutually dependent interests of the two groups, professionals and consumers, with whom he transacts his daily business. Sometimes he is able to do so, sometimes he must take sides. But, always, he has to look out for himself.

Lawyers in private frequently call themselves whores. But just as often they refer to their clients in the same way. There is some evidence for each view.

The client uses the lawyer as a broker and intermediary. For him, counsel means an entree, services guaranteed by an insider who maintains offices "outside" the system. The lawyer is valuable to the client for the purpose of processing the client's affairs through some sort of organization or institution that is, in essence, a bureaucracy—a criminal court, civil court, government agency, or corporation. Always having some particular interest to advance, the client believes the lawyer knows his way around the bureaucracy and can get his goal accomplished.

The lawyer in turn knows that the client's real interest is beyond this bureaucracy. The client's interest may be to get acquitted, vindicate his freedom to smoke pot, recover a money judgment, declare a constitutional right, get a divorce, conduct a business, enter commercial transactions, or avoid deportation. Whatever it is, this interest, if a lawyer has to become involved, must pass through some official, legitimating maze of regulations and restrictions.

The professional concern of any lawyer, then, is first of all to salvage his client's interest. The client pays whatever toll is required for his interest to get through the maze. The lawyer's job is to translate and implement the official requirements for such passage. He is a sort of citizen's guide.

For this reason he has a powerful interest in maintaining the insider-outsider relationship. If simply anyone could negotiate the maze, guides would be out of style or, at least, have a very different status. If the lawyer is an expediter, he must also safeguard the system that requires expediters.

He works for the system in yet another way: as a salesman and recruiter. He and the police—using slightly different means—are its primary sources of customer-referrals. They supply consumers for those services that the law system dispenses, in both the civil and the criminal field. By holding himself out as either necessary or able to make the client's goals legally attainable, the lawyer again serves and preserves the maze.

There are some for whom he cannot do this. Those outside the pale of middle-class beliefs and concerns—because they are too rich, powerful, poor, alienated, or self-contained for the law to have immediate and direct relevance to their daily existence—have very little voluntary professional truck with lawyers. They needn't accept the law as a means for legitimating their ends and accomplishing their goals. If these outer fringes—upper and lower—became too numerous, the present insiders would be stranded, without useful professions or a niche and status for their particular skills. It is in order to preserve the cohesiveness of society that the process of democratization is constant and ongoing, at times sensationally breaking into the immunity of the immensely rich and powerful and at others seeking to dispel the indifference of the very poor—to a point limited, in both cases, by the financial costs and social changes involved.

2

PROFESSIONALS

AT WORK

THE NIGHT before I entered
law practice one of the partners called me at home and said
to stop off at a lower criminal court on my way to the office.
I was to adjourn a hearing scheduled for the first thing in
the morning. Since I had never addressed a client or a
judge, the sudden prospect of doing both in one day, inside
a criminal court, made requesting an adjournment loom like
major litigation. I had contemplated being broken into law
work very gradually. Even after the court layout and every
step of procedure had been painstakingly reviewed, I remained traumatized.

Next morning, clutching an empty briefcase and feeling
damp behind the vest, I entered the building a few minutes
before the calendar call, per instruction, in order to locate
our client. This was magistrates' court (in New York City),

but it seemed to me that it could have been the Fulton Fish Market at 4:00 A.M.—on several counts: crowds, noise, smells. I found the room where he was supposed to be, pushed through its swinging doors, entered the courtroom and boldly called out the word "Gardofsky."

An elderly couple started working their way toward me. One I recognized, from the description I had been given the night before, as our client: conservatively dressed, subdued-looking, a man in his late seventies. "I am Gardofsky," he said.

We moved to one side. I introduced myself as "from your lawyer's office," shook hands, and turned to the woman who had come up with him. "Mrs. Gardofsky?" I inquired, smiling. "No," she said. "I am the complainant, his downstairs neighbor. I have no lawyer. I don't need one. Mr. Gardofsky and me came here together. Now I am expecting two witnesses. One is the landlady."

With this kind of rapport between adversaries, my task now seemed like a pushover. Immediately, I explained my mission. Gardofsky nodded one way, his opponent the other. "I know what you're up to," she said. "Absolutely no adjournments, no more."

The judge was announced. Everyone was ordered to stand up. Those with seats started sitting down again as soon as he entered and began making his way to the bench. He settled into a rickety, cracked-leather, high-backed swivel recliner and twirled around twice. The court officer spoke again: "Find seats. Find seats, everybody. Put away all newspapers and magazines. AND STOP THE TALKING!" There were no empty seats. Along with about sixty others, we stayed in the side aisle.

The complainant continued. "This is my fourth time here" —a wrinkle my boss had overlooked explaining. "I can't take it any more. He's impossible up there." She spoke clearly over the din, without anger.

A square-looking woman seemed to be elbowing her way toward us through the standees and was waving to the complainant. The latter turned to me. "Here comes the landlady." When the square woman came up, she spoke at once. "I'm the landlady. Never another adjournment. I offer him a better apartment. One on the ground floor. But he won't take it."

"Quiet in the courtroom," the officer yelled. "Find seats, everyone. You, in the back row, TAKE THAT HAT OFF!" There was nothing to do but wait until the case was called.

When it was, we all stood behind a table facing the bench. I tried to remember my script. "Judge," I began, "Mr. Simon is handling this case. I'm not familiar with the file at all. In fact, I don't even have one. Unfortunately, Mr. Simon's not available, and we're asking for about two weeks—"

The landlady burst in. "Three times here before, judge. I'm the landlady and he's ruining my house and business. What's he cut holes in the floor for? Big ones he drills—"

The complainant took over. "Judge, he pours water down them onto my rug, at two in the morning. Or lies on the floor and stares at me through the holes. I can't live."

"Your honor," I said. "This seems to be a fantastic and serious matter and—"

I got no farther. "Mark it ready for a hearing. Get ready counselor," the judge said, squinting at my client. "After the calendar call."

I took Gardofsky into the crowded hallway outside the courtroom. "What's the story," I asked. "Do you do those things?"

The man looked at me intensely. "Have to," he said. "It's

the 'eye' down there. Once I can extinguish it, I'm all right. But it keeps moving around. I haven't hit it yet. So I've got to keep watch. I can't sleep." He paused for a moment. "And that's why I can't take the ground floor, although it's nice of her to offer. It wouldn't be safe. The 'eye,' " he said, gently, "could get me."

The landlady and complainant had come into the hall nearby. I told Gardofsky to stay put, took them to one side and asked if they knew why he drilled holes, poured water down them and then kept his vigil. They both said yes. "He's been with us fifteen years," the landlady added. "Four years ago his brother died. They used to live together. And then a year ago he started with the 'eye.' "

"He's a nice man, otherwise," the complainant added. "Where could he go? That's why we want him in the building. But he should be on the ground floor. Maybe you can get him to take it?"

I phoned the office. From the booth I kept a watch on the client, who didn't budge from where I left him. He looked straight ahead, serenely oblivious to the hubbub around him. Neither partner was in the office.

Feeling a little desperate, I returned to the client. "Look, Mr. Gardofsky, how about that other apartment just for awhile?" He looked at me patiently. "Can't, don't you see?"

Another thought crossed my mind. A magistrate had discretionary power to order the defendant in a criminal case to Bellevue Hospital for preliminary psychiatric observation. "Mr. Gardofsky," I said. "The judge can get you out of the building entirely. Maybe if you go to a hospital the 'eye' will be gone when you get out. It would be only for a few weeks. The landlady doesn't want you in jail. Your downstairs neighbor doesn't. And we don't." He looked at me for what must have been a minute. "If you really think," he said, "that it could be gone."

When the case was called again, I got permission to approach the bench. "Judge, this man tells me he did these things in order to extinguish some kind of 'eye' in the woman's apartment downstairs. He thinks it's after him. He doesn't seem dangerous and I'm requesting observation."

I resumed my place behind the table. The judge made his statement "for the record": "After conference with the defendant's attorney, and upon his request, I am remanding this defendant to Bellevue for observation."

Gardofsky didn't look unhappy. The last I ever saw of him was a rear view, an erect old man walking toward the door behind the judge's bench that led to detention cells. He was dwarfed by the uniformed department of correction guard who held it ajar.

When I finally made contact with the partners and recounted the story to them, neither was horrified. One said it was "good work and fast thinking." The other reacted more philosophically: "The guy's a nut, right? So that's where he belongs, right?"

About a month later Mr. Simon, one of my partners, appeared in court on the case and the judge then presiding granted an additional thirty days for observation because the doctors hadn't gotten around to Gardofsky yet. In another month the case was on again. A different judge heard the complaint and read the medical summary that had been readied. To my best recollection, Simon's view of the ensuing conference—among landlady, complainant, judge, and him (who, like myself, was of course Gardofsky's representative)—went something like this:

"This landlady gets a choice: take Gardofsky back or help put him away permanently. The judge promises to scare hell out of the guy if she'll take him in. She's fed up with court and worn out from visits to Bellevue. So she won't come back for any more. Gardofsky looks pretty dazed, too, after two months in the bin. The judge gets him in front of the bench and says he's going to send him back to the hospital forever or put him in jail for a long time if he doesn't stop his nonsense, then asks if he knows how serious a charge it is and is he going to quit with the holes and water. By now he doesn't know anything, but Gardofsky answers 'yes' quick. The judge tells the complainant if she has any more trouble to come back immediately, so she agrees to drop the charges. Just to make sure the whole thing keeps out of court, he gets them to decide that *she* belongs two floors down, in the ground-floor apartment that Gardofsky won't take. And Gardofsky's not going to live forever."

This case remains vivid for reasons other than that it launched my career. It illustrates some fundamental operations of the law as well as an example of shrewd and brilliant jurisprudence from-the-hip.

To begin, there is the court process itself, no different here than in millions of other instances. The key to this process is that it absorbs time, pre-empts schedules, and takes away a sense of the participants' control over their own destinies. It injects into controversy the uncertainty of a judicial personality, the possibility that either side's equities will be misunderstood in the process of being presented, and a system of making decisions according to principles that may be alien or seem irrelevant to those looking for support of their interests.

A significant part of the court's function depends on this basic inefficiency, inconvenience, and incomprehensibility. Litigants come to feel helplessly passive within the workings of an alien machinery. This feeling begins a softening-up process that disposes them to want out before their die is cast in an all-or-nothing showdown and makes them more responsive to advice from their guides, the lawyers. Poised for compromise, each litigant begins looking for the optimal time to get out. This time comes when the likelihood of any further advantage seems outweighed by the further strain of remaining in. At some point, all sides' private interests in disengaging from the court process intersect.

The judge's job is to find this point. His object is to effect a forced accommodation of people to the system. Gardofsky, for example, had been beaten down by his experiences in the ward. His landlady had finally to choose between gratifying her affection and maternal instincts, on the one hand, and symbolically avenging a property loss and her sense of being abused, on the other. The downstairs neighbor had to relocate in order to gain her primary objective of surcease from prying eyes and poured pitchersful. Although objectively, this solution had been one of her options before she started the lawsuit, it became a feasible one only after the magistrate anointed her cause and offered the empty assurance that she could later pick up her case where it was being left off. (Obviously if Gardofsky could no longer bother her because of her move, there would be no occasion to revive the case. Any further aberrations that might be directed against a new tenant could be the subject only of a different lawsuit, begun anew.) Gardofsky's agreement to call a halt to his actions could not have been coerced out of him so easily before he got a taste of confinement, abuse, and, probably, brutality. The landlady could not be brought round to a settlement until she had wasted hours in court and faced the further prospect of becoming involved in an unpleasant and prolonged commitment procedure, from which she would gain nothing in furtherance of her basic interests.

The case could have been resolved by the parties themselves, on exactly the same terms, except that a court and judge were required to bring into the picture a sense of final authority, the feeling that the end of the road had been reached. The ritual of law created the appearance that society had some appropriate means up its sleeve for dealing with a Gardofsky—which it does not—a way to change his behavior and police the change. To the extent that those involved accepted this appearance for reality, their belief became self-fulfilling.

My own self-protective maneuver to get Gardofsky out of the way lubricated the machinery of Justice. I suspected at the time—and experience confirmed—that I was volunteering the client for a fate worse than jail. Even if he had gone to trial on the spot and lost, no judge would have sent him to prison, much less for two months. Without a lawyer, his case could have ended as it finally did, minus its confinement feature, with the judge sending everyone home on a threat and a prayer.

Although the client's well-being seemed to justify my request for his psychiatric observation, my actual motivation was to save my own skin. Relying on the shield of law's proclaimed intent not to punish those who are "irresponsible" and its official processes for making this determination, I could gloss over the reality of Bellevue's horrors to which, in essence, I sentenced my own client. What I was doing was "making a record," a technique that amounts to pretending to take selected facts on face value.

The judge was doing the same. None of the stated purposes for a pyschiatric observation really applied. Gardofsky, his landlady, his neighbor, his lawyer, and the judge were in perfect agreement about what he had done. We all concurred about his reasons. Except for him, all felt that this behavior was irrational—and his judgment didn't count. The question was: had he exceeded the limits of tolerance that determine normalcy? The answer had to be "yes," not because he was seeing an "eye" but because he was drilling holes, pouring water, and keeping watch. Whatever the Bellevue psychiatrists would find, if anything, about his judgment in other respects could bear no relevance to our conclusion and certainly could not alter it. All that could change what we already believed and "knew" to be the fact was an inspection of the downstairs apartment that would reveal an "eye" actually there. This the psychiatrists were surely not going to undertake. *Their* sole function was to do a re-write job on Gardofsky's own story, as he had already told it. They would then submit their version back to the judge, who had sent Gardofsky to them in the first place.

The psychological grace-notes of the narrative would show that they had done their own thing—administered tests, conducted interviews, and collected legally useless demographic information about the defendant. These were in one sense irrelevant because it is not officially a crime to have a certain IQ, a particular ethnic background, or to fall within or without a standard deviation on some psychological test. Information of this sort could neither prove nor disprove the "eye's" existence. So the report would confirm what the fact of referral told the psychiatrists the judge already believed—simply stated, that Gardofsky was nuts. But if the psychiatrists did not respond to the judge's cues and repeat what they knew he wanted to hear, they themselves would become suspect and, if they remained recalcitrant in many such cases, they would lose their usefulness in the judicial process. The purpose of the psychiatrists' report was simply to get written. Their writing could then become part of a record and sanction the threat, or actual implementation, of a particular legal option—that of putting Gardofsky in a mental institution.

The real relevance of the referral was to give the judge something to do. It saved, first of all, his own judicial skin. The authority of law was preserved because something was done at the proceeding other than granting a fourth adjournment. Because the litigants before the judge had not yet reached the point of exhaustion that would prompt them to bow out of the proceedings altogether, their case was not yet ripe for voluntary settlement. If it had proceeded to trial, the judge could exercise only a coercive rather than an apparently consensual option. None of his choices would have been as happy as the solution finally made possible after I stepped in and obligingly took everyone, except Gardofsky, off the hook.

Before Gardofsky returned from Bellevue, an all-parties compromise was not on the horizon. If the judge had simply granted another adjournment, he would have lost a quantum of consumer faith in his legal system. An important part of his job in every case is to safeguard this faith, if possible, while getting rid of essentially unsolvable human problems. Generating activity within the system successfully meets the challenge of appearing responsive despite the fact that there may be no logical or legal connection between what is being ordered and the elements of the conflict to be resolved. In Gardofsky's case, court personnel and those in an allied bureaucracy, the hospital prison ward, became activated and occupied. The litigants, who had submitted a specific problem for decision, were put in the position of learning the lesson that they had better accept a settlement soon or things might get worse. By just doing something, the judge prepared them for accepting the law's parlor trick of settlement as legal magic. He and I shored each other up and perpetuated the image of our own and the other's necessary functions by playing a law game and drawing the audience into it as actor-participants.

The Gardofsky case, because of its simplicity, is useful as an illustration of certain constant relationships between client, lawyer, judge, and legal institutions. But the inherent conflicts-of-interests that it points up, and the legal operations it reveals, are not confined to neophyte lawyers, criminal courts, senile clients and "minor," isolated or bizarre incidents.

3

ON THE

WATERFRONT

WHEN THE cop approached my car I explained that I was waiting for a passenger. "Obstructing the pier entrance," he said. "You can't stay here. My orders are to keep it open. Besides, passengers won't be off for another hour."

A block away, the middle of the street under the West Side Highway was painted with about twenty parking spaces. Two large signs dangled from a rope fence: CUSTOMS OFFICIALS ONLY and TOW-AWAY ZONE. The cop motioned toward the customs lot. "Pull over there," he said. "For an hour I won't bother you and if the tow truck comes I'll tell them you're waiting."

I thanked him for being helpful. As I turned to look, I noticed a closer area—also on the street, painted and roped-off. It was only about half-filled with cars. A sign said:

LONGSHOREMEN ONLY. "How about there?" I asked. "It's closer."

The officer scowled. "Mister," he said, "you gotta be kidding. If you parked there, there wouldn't be enough left to tow away. Maybe the car gets set on fire—or the windows are smashed, your motor's busted and the tires gone. *They* gotta have a place to park," he added, by way of explanation. "It's their *job!*"

Meeting that passenger could also have been my job. But the cop was protecting my property, I had to admit. For I was getting from him an incredibly frank disclosure to the effect that he, in fact the whole police force, turned their backs on whatever gangsterism happened on a portion of public land that had been informally ceded to longshoremen. That particular turf was left entirely to the workings of private law. The understanding that gave longshoremen sovereignty over these approximately 1,000-square-yards was so overt that the necessity of maintaining an illusion of official enforcement there—from ticketing or towing to preventing the destruction of property, and possibly more—had been abandoned.

Still, police at the pier had a definite task in helping to sustain this sovereignty. They were paid from city funds to warn the general public that a private government was enforcing its own law on the premises. This aspect of their job served to minimize the costs a union might spend for paramilitary, strong-arm services: if a "free" watchman did his job, the number of "necessary" crimes that would have to be committed in order to protect their turf could be minimized and, if he were vivid enough, words alone might suffice. In that sense, police were deterring and preventing crime. They maintained order by acknowledging and assisting a power group to which public authority had become subordinate.

A watchman's position, with overtones of public relations, was a very demanding role for the cop at the pier. The judgments that he had to make, according to his own sense of priorities, frequently called for an instantaneous assessment of conflicts that might potentially explode the established balance between various forces and interests. None of the rules by which a cop could be guided in resolving these conflicts was official; on the other hand, none of the official rules that ostensibly govern a policeman's conduct had much relevance. Should misjudgments occur, his own neck would be in a noose because full disclosure of what was actually at play—even if he really understood and could formulate what was going on—would have to be disowned by the authorities.

The job required fast wits and fancy footwork, which the working conditions made feasible: the cop had professional elbow-room. As the only representative of official authority on the scene, his decisions were likely to be respected as final, if only because the stakes were so very low and any appeal to the next highest authority required a tremendous expenditure of time and energy by an aggrieved party. The cop was a small-claims court unto himself. And more, as we shall see.

But what was he really put on the job to accomplish? In the three hours that it took to complete docking and all disembarking ceremonies, I made some observations. Aside from serving as a symbol—just being there—and keeping the longshoremen's space cleared, he was primarily concerned with supervising lawbreaking and permitting offenders to function under "color of the law." His job, in essence, was the orderly enforcement of illegality.

From among a sparse handful of illegal alternatives that were available, he made balanced choices according to what seemed to him to be demanded in a situation geared toward one single priority: expediting the flow of people and cars—impediments of official law to the contrary notwithstanding. Under the circumstances that he faced, enforcing the literal law would have meant human and economic chaos. But it was not an alternative that seemed to have occurred to him.

He accomplished his appointed task with fascinating dexterity. Some vehicles were dispatched to the customs lot, others sent to doublepark here or there, a select few allowed to block the pier entrance, and many others directed to line the officially forbidden feeder streets that led to the pier. One of his most creative maneuvers was redirecting several cars that had independently parked parallel to a waterside curb—which was liberally bedecked with TOW-AWAY and NO-STANDING-AT-ANY-TIME signs—to new, angled parking positions. Thereby, he increased illegal-curbing capacity three-fold.

Throughout, he appeared guided by a sense of traffic justice that transcended law, one that was based, instead, on a combination of common sense, first-come-first-served fundamentalism, snap judgments about who looked more important—or less argumentative—than whom, necessity (a particular car-and-trailer combination, for example, could fit into only one spot and was directed there), and fast decisions about "hardship" cases involving, variously, a man who said he was meeting a lady with three infants ("okay, stay here"), a driver whose passenger was on crutches (ditto), and a young traveller with an unusual amount of luggage to be unloaded ("sorry mac, that's the law; you'll have to move out").

As the situation grew more frantic, he became increasingly efficient, showing what seemed to be exactly the right mixture of authoritarianism, humaneness, cajolery, and indignation for each case handled. Now he was functioning as judge, jury, prosecutor, chief witness and appeals court, all rolled into one—without clerks or staff of any sort. In exercising his appellate function in at least one case, he overruled his own earlier decision on the basis of vehement logic being advanced from a driver's seat.

The status and authority of that cop at the pier derived from the convergence of various interests and sources of power. Their relationship with each other are fairly typical of what goes on in many different kinds of situations when law is enforced.

The official law, expressed on posted signs, made it amply clear that only selected cars were allowed to park or stand on land within the cop's immediate domain, under his "jurisdiction." Both the letter and the spirit of official law made it mandatory for him to evacuate all cars except those belonging to longshoremen and customs inspectors. Neither his departmental rules nor the relevant laws—in this case, the state's *Vehicle and Traffic Law* and the city's *Traffic Regulations*—gave him any alternative to enforcing the rules as posted.

Yet just the opposite was happening.

In the situation on the piers, the law obviously could not be enforced literally unless the steamship companies—and their associated economy, including the union—were to be closed down. Such a radical and disruptive decision certainly would not be initiated by a low-level operative like the officer on the beat. Instead, he naturally assumed that his superiors' and the public's expectations were that he would continue the precedent, or safe practice, routinized over decades, of protecting commerce by speeding an "illegal" traffic flow. It is unlikely that any thought would cross the enforcer's mind suggesting that his duty included volunteering for the part of St. George against the powerful twin dragons of an international union and the international shipping industry in the nation's major port. The power, real or imagined, of either labor or industry to destroy him professionally or obliterate him physically would discourage any such idea from germinating, even if its seed existed. His job was to enforce priorities determining the permissible private use of public land that had long ago been resolved in anonymous councils.

So the cop was *interpreting and applying the law,* in this situation, according to the interests of private commerce. This interest was so entrenched that to the unaided eye it was invisible. Despite the domineering physical presence of business—the giant pier apparatus and operations—enforcement created the impression of being only a matter between individual citizens and the policeman on the scene. There was no visible link to the shipping companies or the union—such as, for example, open orders from the dock boss or a company executive. These contacts, if they existed, occurred on a higher level. Probably the desk sergeant did not have to remind the cop setting forth from the station house to discharge his duties at the pier by ignoring the posted law. Everyone "knew" what was expected without hearing it spoken in so many words. Both union and shippers undoubtedly disdained as unnecessary the giving of serious bribes to these police sentries, who could be counted as their first-line private army. Because of the enormity of their physical, political, and financial interests, they were unlike small shopkeepers plagued with the necessity of constant payoffs to every visiting inspector or moseying patrolman assigned to the beat. Business protection was simply an inherent police priority, the birthright of power.

But another interest had to be accommodated as a part of the established order: that of ordinary citizens who briefly shared a common concern for getting themselves, their cars, and their cargos safely through the vehicular stampede that took place before and after docking. So long as their ends could be accomplished, these citizens would remain uninterested, or at least uninvolved, in who ran the piers and how the law was interpreted there. Although too transiently constituted to be a "group" in any strict sense of the word, if stymied they could—and probably would—bring to bear all the resources and influence that were available to individual members of the upper and middle classes. The police had to apply to these citizens different tactics than might be used in dealing with, say, a band of student demonstrators, or else risk the possibility of repercussions in the press or political repercussions behind the scenes. The interests of the dock visitors had to be accommodated efficiently and with a minimum of discomfort.

In this case, the interests of the travelling public and of shippers and the union actually converged. Both could be satisfied by similar police actions. It is necessary, however, to keep in mind an important difference between the two— their relative power.

As a class, travellers had only a fleeting concern for how things were done at the pier. They can be labeled *ostensible* consumers of police legal services. Most were one- or two-time ship's visitors and, therefore, unfamiliar with details of "normal" operation and actual procedures. Their expectations were not well defined. In the event of unusual occurrences or delays they would tend to be slow to recognize or react when their concerns did not receive priority attention.

Moreover, since the pier was not part of their daily routine, most had probably allowed themselves a fair amount of time to complete their business there or, at least, had contingency plans to enable them to meet the unexpected without too much disruption. Their frame of reference made it possible for them to look on these experiences as an adventure, an entertainment or, at most, an inconvenience worth recounting along with other travel stories. They could, thus, tolerate considerable manipulation without being roused to a pitch of indignation that would result in their taking steps that might jeopardize the waterfront status quo.

By contrast, shipping and union interests were permanent. When the cop shrugged off longshoremen crime with the explanation that "*They* have to do it; it's their job!" he did not mean to imply that the necessity of making a living excused crime (as he defined it). Rather, he was rationalizing his professional acceptance of a power that seemed greater than his own in this one small enclave. Since labor and business were the ones who "paid the piper"—or, at least, called his tune—we may fairly regard them as *controlling* consumers of police legal services.

Their investment in operations at the pier were, of course, far greater than any single traveller's. Their joint resources for controlling the operation were concentrated and far-reaching, in fact, and overwhelmingly so compared to the scattered and diffuse potential of individuals who picked up or delivered passengers and then went about their unrelated businesses. Labor and industry alike, because of a continuing and vital association with the waterfront, were highly motivated to use their power to protect the existing system and defend their prerogative to implement whatever changes they decided comprised their interests.

That, in this situation, the interests of *ostensible* and *con-*

trolling consumers largely coincided—that travellers were more or less served—constituted a sort of inferential fiction that the police, in serving labor and industry, were also serving the "general" public. Actually, however, this tenuous harmony of interests was artificially controlled. Competing interests of the public were simply not represented in the cauldron of forces in which decisions about the piers were compounded.

One might imagine a host of questions being asked by the representatives of the public at a council on the operations of the pier. Was it more important for longshoremen than for anyone else to drive to work and park free? Why were they granted a proprietary right over a public street, one excluding all other usage of that land? Should shippers receive private services of the police in order to help manage their flow of customers and maintain their privileges?

Such questions, without ever being formally posed, were answered—pragmatically. Instead of arising from conscious deliberations in any forum, the answers were operational ones, force vectors that had been derived through usage and the exercise of power sanctified by habit and precedent. Among the interests of police, travellers, labor, and industry, there were no significant conflicts, only differing priorities.

But what about the law—the official, written law—and those activities that constituted its enforcement?

In a sense, both signs and the police served the same purpose: *to warn and inform the public.* But in this case, as in many others, the warning and information were contradictory. Signs declared in words what conduct was illegal. They were the written law. A police uniform was another kind of sign—nonverbal, a symbol conveying the message that a particular enforcement mechanism, the cop, was then and there representing official society. Thus, what he and not the signs said became effective law at the time. He was the law's spokesman. What he endorsed, tolerated, or directed amounted to functional legality. Those who accepted his interpretations received the protection of authority: immunity from harassment and prosecution.

Picture a line-up of cars on the pier, their "law-abiding" drivers awaiting their turn to be officially directed, by a policeman, to every imaginable nook and cranny of an area peppered with signs that say NO PARKING and threaten violators with the punishment of being towed away. The cop in such a situation functioned somewhat like a priest— except that he was offering absolution in advance, for violations about to be committed. By taking charge, he incriminated the whole legal establishment and, thus, implicitly removed the threat of prosecution that is the practical definition of any criminal act. His participation turned illegal parking into a nonoffense in the same way that an army chaplain's benedictions on the eve of battle give the sanction of religion to murder. Most cars were soon emptied, their drivers entering onto the pier. This indicated their firm reliance on the cop's implied representation that they would not find their vehicles either ticketed or towed away if they did what he said.

This tells us something important about the ordinary citizen's relationship to the legal system. The law of the signs became outmoded by a set of unscrutinized assumptions and expectations that came to be accepted as a matter of course: first, a city that accepted a shipping operation of major proportions would also provide some workable arrangement for luggage and passengers; second, some sort of bargain had been struck with the law that guaranteed immunity from the kind of harassment or prosecution that, under these circumstances, would not be "fair."

It may have seemed that the cop was, after all, only legitimating the inevitable. Although this was, in fact, the case, still, each driver had to make his own independent assessment of the situation. What would the cop have to do in order to enforce the law effectively, within a short time, against several hundred drivers? How serious was the violation that he was licensing them to commit? Did he have sufficient control and authority to deliver on his promise of immunity? What would be the likely consequences, to him, of trying seriously to enforce the law? What was the risk— for cop and driver alike?

Fairly obviously, the posted law was a tool of control that actually facilitated, not prevented, parking. It was intended and used for a purpose exactly opposite to the one stated in words. Changeable and changing conditions at the pier required a means by which one individual would have authority to make decisions on the spot. Signs, then, were a device for conferring this authority in order to regulate parking, to *restrict* not prevent it. Any cop would know that he was expected to use the law only against those who failed to obey orders. Signs were necessary to make these orders lawful because, without them, anyone could park anywhere, any time. The area could not then be reserved for shipping customers unless leased by the companies. Like the cop himself, the signs were a free offering that excluded the "wrong" people. They were intended to be disobeyed—but selectively and under the "safe" supervision of the police. Once put up, they legitimated the cop's role and it then became his job, in turn, to supersede them.

This use of the law is fairly common, if not characteristic, in a whole variety of enforcement situations. It sheds light on the real nature of written statutes. They should not be understood as meaning what they purport to say, even after having been interpreted in court. They can be properly considered only if one examines the interaction between the stated law and the particular interests that are being served by it—in actual setting. Otherwise, we miss entirely the seven-eighths of the iceberg that is below the surface.

4

COPS

AND LAWYERS

¶ THE RULES OF THE GAME

I had been told that my client's life would be endangered if he were subjected to unusual tension. Waiting in court would produce just the kind of anxiety that might bring on another incapacitating, or even fatal, stroke. He was suing for damages sustained in an automobile accident several years back precisely on the grounds that the crash had caused one major stroke and made him highly susceptible to others. Because of certain unusual tactics that had been used earlier to delay progress of the case and other tactics that now had the effect of making it even more difficult than usual to estimate when we might begin to pick a jury, I

firmly believed that my adversary was engineering circumstances that would increase the likelihood of my client's not
living through trial.

As a counter-measure to protect him from unnecessary
emotional pressures, I decided that the client should not
leave home even when his jury had been selected. For even
then the case might be delayed another week because of
factors such as the length of time it took to complete earlier
trials, the availability of judges, the clerk's particular
method of selecting "ready, jury-picked" cases for trial, or
some unexpected change in my adversary's schedule.

As soon as the case was actually assigned to a specific
judge and courtroom, I planned to telephone the client.
Then he and his wife would begin their three-hour drive
into the state.

Although this arrangement was the best I could devise, it
meant taking a calculated risk. After picking a jury, it was
possible that, instead of waiting, we would immediately be
sent to a trial part—or room—and told to begin at once. If
I didn't have a starting witness, the judge would probably
be unwilling to recess. He would discharge the jury and
send the case back to the "assignment" part, where the
whole process of waiting to pick another jury and then waiting to be reassigned to another trial judge and courtroom
would begin again. We would be at the end of a line of
cases also waiting their turn, and the client would be en
route, beyond recall.

I met this problem of orchestration by selecting as my
prospective lead-off witness the cop who had arrived at the
scene shortly after the accident occurred. He agreed to
come to court each morning. If I were sent to pick a jury, he
would remain in court throughout the selection process and
until the case was actually reached for trial.

In explaining the importance of his appearing in court every day, I had to make sure that he understood the timing that was proposed. I would prolong the inevitable preliminary conference in the judge's chambers, make an expanded "opening statement" to the jury, and then stretch out his own testimony. If the client still had not appeared, I would need only a short recess and could explain that my infirm plaintiff had already been on the road for several hours. Counting on sympathy and the judge's being caught up in the momentum of midtrial, I thought it fairly safe to assume that he would be willing to await the client's momentary arrival—if the situation arose.

We were, however, still far from that point. For the past week I had appeared in court daily, answered the call of the assignment calendar, and daily learned that I would not be reached to pick a jury that day. Every morning, "John"— the officer, with whom I was now on a first-name basis— duly appeared and waited the hour or so it took for me to become officially informed of the impossibility of picking a jury. Then, routinely, I told him that he wouldn't be needed until the next day. A ritual soon developed. We adjourned to a "greasy-spoon" diner near the court; there I sipped coffee and bought him bacon and eggs. In half-an-hour, John would leave for his precinct, I for my office.

It originally came as something of a shock to me to realize that getting the client's serious case into a courtroom hung in large measure on the delicate thread of my being able to enlist the continuing sympathy of this clean-cut young man who didn't look a day older than twenty-five—and who had no real stake in what happened.

When I met John for the first time, the thought crossed my mind that he should be playing the honeymooner in a daytime television serial. At any rate, he surely seemed miscast in his present role, a plainclothes detective working out of the Public Morals Division of the New York City Police Department. At the time of the accident, he and a partner were riding a patrol car. Since then he had become a veteran specialist in numbers and policy arrests.

By the third morning—having exhausted the amenities, shared our thoughts about living on Long Island, compared criminal with civil trials, and discussed the medical and legal aspects of my client's case—the conversation got around to John's work. It began cautiously. Because of the importance of his continuing to make daily appearances, I treaded lightly at first. We both knew that no subpoena could command the degree of cooperation that I needed. Previously I had offered to reimburse him for any "expenses" that he might have in going to court "on his own time," but this topic had been gallantly waived until after the trial. In any event, money would be unlikely to sway his actions should he decide that I was "anti-cop."

By the fifth morning, however, things had changed. The conversation was freer on both sides, extending now to his opinion of lawyers. Perhaps he was reciprocating the frankness with which I had shared my plight about getting the trial started. Or maybe it was only that so many successive brunches bred familiarity. Whatever the reason, he was obviously enjoying the opportunity to chastise one of a breed he considered responsible for "increased crime and the bad reputation that cops have." In exchange, he seemed equally willing to enter a no-holds-barred discussion about the police. I soon understood why so many lawyers became friendly enemies with cops. It was a relief to reach so easily the point in relationships where both sides abandon their professional veneer as unnecessary.

We were discussing narcotics and numbers cases. "The problem isn't lawyers," I said, "but that too many cops make 'plants.' " I was referring to stories I often heard from clients about how the arresting officer "found" the evidence in their possession. "So many people who don't know each other aren't just happening to be telling me the same lie," I said.

He flashed the same boyish TV grin that I had found so reassuring for five mornings running as I arrived in court. "I'll tell you how it is," he said. "Sure I make plants, we all do, but I only do it when I have to and it's right. I never plant on someone who I don't know is guilty. For example, I've just busted in and there's this guy with a list of numbers in his mouth. There's no doubt that he's guilty. And he's ready to swallow. If he does, I won't have a 'collar' [an arrest] if I go by the rules. But he won't have his numbers, either. I know the one thing he wants is those numbers. He's got to have them for payoffs or else he's dead on the street. Everybody will be making claims against him and he won't have any proof. For my part, I don't want some 'coon's' rabies, a handful of spit, or my hands chewed to pieces.

"So I make a deal," he continued. "I say: 'Look, you need those numbers. If you swallow you won't have them and I'm gonna put some on you, anyway. I've got 'em right here in my pocket. But just hand them over and I'll let you make a copy and put it somewhere safe.' Believe me," he went on, "most of them take it, they trust me and know I'm telling the truth. They're grateful. But in the rare case when the guy swallows, then I can't just let him walk away."

"Why not?" I asked. "What difference does it make? Does being a cop include committing crimes and then perjuring yourself?" I wondered whether this question would be considered beyond the rules. It wasn't. John just turned on his smile, bound and determined to make me understand airtight logic.

"For two reasons," he answered. "First a cop is supposed to prevent crime. I wouldn't be doing my job. Here I see this guy with what we both know is a list. You can't let them get away with it or you've lost all your self-respect and they'll never respect you. Remember, I'm going to see this fellow again, and his friends will find out. You get known." He turned to the second reason. "Next, there's the captain. If he sees that you're not making as many collars as you used to or that you're the lowest in the squad, what's he going to think? That you're on the make. You can get into trouble that way."

After a moment's pause, he continued: "I'll admit that not every cop is like this." John was going to round off the picture. "You get some guys," he said, "especially older men, who are just lazy, like in any job. They don't care any more. They won't even try—just walk up to someone they know plays the numbers and take him in. They have a few slips ready. But don't judge us all by them," he added, sincerely. "In every barrel there are some rotten apples."

¶ MAKING THE LAW WORK: COPS

John's comments and behavior illustrate some of the many ways in which the acts and outlooks of lawyers and cops parallel each other. Some of their professional conflicts and interests are similar, and many others are reciprocal. Both have in common an ideological commitment to serving and achieving Justice. Both are steeped in an amorphous identification with "the law," heavily indoctrinated with the idea that their function is to work within, support, uphold, enforce, and advance it.

But "it" is an abstraction. What lawyers and cops deal with every day is bureaucracy, an apparatus consisting of procedures and consequences. Its structure is made up in part of written and unwritten rules that are applied, enforced, and interpreted by individuals assigned specific decision-making tasks within the bureaucracy. In discharging their professional duties, these individuals, as bureaucrats, interpret and make judgmental decisions not only about written and unwritten rules but also about the actions of others. Even apparently routine and ministerial aspects of their jobs are "judicial" in the sense that they require the exercise of ethical and value discretion and an anticipatory reaction to judgments that might probably be made by others on the way they exercised this discretion. Sometimes they pass judgment on fellow bureaucrats, sometimes on individuals entirely outside the official law bureaucracy.

John's discourse described some important aspects of his relationship with both groups of people.

With respect to outsiders, there was his invention of an individual poised to ingest a piece of paper that had names and numbers written on it. Now this man was, in effect, John's "customer," the kind of person with whom he had specialized professional dealings. John's job as a hunter required him to penetrate a defined area of the city and find such men. It was clear from his remarks that he had been able to obtain this access, the first requisite of his work: making contact with potential customers.

This accomplished, John then had to absorb his contact into the bureaucracy in order to commence the process of criminalizing him. John's was the first link in a chain of activities specifically concerned with the criminalizing process by which a nonlabeled citizen is transformed into one with the special status of "defendant." This status has consequences for the defendant, insiders of the law bureaucracy, and everyone outside the official bureaucracy with whom the defendant at any time afterward has dealings.

In carrying out his professional duties of criminalizing his contacts, John had to make judgments and interpretations about certain rules guiding the process. He had to assign priorities among potentially conflicting instructions. The results with which he ended up had to be rationalized in a way that enabled him to accept morally all the actions that he was called upon to perform. Somehow, he had to regard his actions as consistent within themselves and as "right." There were several alternatives open to him in making critical decisions.

John knew that if the criminalizing process were to be completed—if an arrest was to become a conviction—the rules of evidence required his possession of a paper such as he described, a numbers or policy slip. Other rules required him to make a statement about the relationship between this paper and the person he had selected to make a defendant—in order to establish "possession," in other words, to connect the arrested person with the evidence. This relationship could be proven, on the record, in certain ways— for example, by his saying he had personally observed the defendant with the paper in his pocket (or mouth). But it would be legally insufficient if John tried to establish this connection by saying other things—for example, that he personally had not seen anything, but simply had heard that the defendant booked or played numbers. As "hearsay," this testimony would be excluded. In sum, the paper needed to have certain characteristics, and John's statement about its relationship to the defendant could include words only to a certain effect.

At a trial he would be called on to describe how he first got the evidence. If he presented his story in a certain way —saying, for example, that he planted the paper in the defendant's pocket and then took it out and made the arrest— the "seizure" of evidence wouldn't count, that is, it would be deemed "unconstitutional." This version would have the consequence of annulling all of John's professional efforts— and someone who he "knew" was "guilty" would escape conviction! (If, during the trial, John admitted the plant, he himself would be declared criminal; but if, as a result of doubts cast on his veracity on cross examination or after the defendant's own testimony, a judge or jury believed that John had taken the evidence illegally, there would then be no official action against him but the defendant would nevertheless be acquitted.)

Further, the defendant might be acquitted unless John testified to a "chain of possession." He would have to say that he had safeguarded the evidence from the time he acquired it until it was presented in court, thus eliminating "for the record" the possibility of its having been tampered with in the interim.

Like most cops, John was interested in more than just arrests. He had many reasons to be vitally concerned that at least a certain percentage of his arrests became convictions. Internal organizational pressures required that his time be averagely "productive." A significant discrepancy between his and other officers' arrest-conviction ratios would indicate that he must be doing something wrong.

As he stated, it might indicate inefficiency or suggest the possibility that he was taking bribes. If John's records showed a conspicuous disparity between arrests and convictions, either inference would be a reasonable one. Information would be available to John's captain, who would then come under pressure to act in any one of several ways, regardless of his professional opinion about whether the discrepancy meant anything at all. The captain would be concerned about covering *him*self in the event of a future investigation into how he handled this information.

It is axiomatic that all police bribes are shared upward at least to the level of command having control over the immediate contact officer. The captain, therefore, would risk falling under suspicion unless there was on John's record a fairly constant number of convictions that could be pointed to as "normal"—should the unwanted occasion of an investigation ever arise. Like any member of an organization, John knew that his bread was not buttered on the side of exposing his boss to embarrassment, a possibly awkward situation, or, most serious of all, an indictment. So he needed x-number of arrests to protect the boss.

Finally, there was the matter of John's own professional pride. As an officer sensitive to the criticism that cops closed their eyes to crime, as someone occupationally committed to the ideal of catching crooks, and as a citizen personally concerned with the same alarms that affected everybody else, John's sense of Justice was outraged when someone whom he was assured was guilty escaped prosecution. This outrage was compounded when it was John's own actions that permitted the escape, his own case.

For all these reasons, then, a cop is under strong pressure to keep up with the Joneses at work and adhere to the operational norms of the police force. This pressure exists regardless of whether he is unlucky, guilty of sloppy police-work, dishonest, unpersuasive in court, or simply an example of the principle of random selection.

John was at least a typical cop who "knew the score." His skills, experience, special education, and police training all converged to make him sophisticated about the rules of the law bureaucracy. He had to become as knowledgeable as he could about these rules because it formed the milieu of his operation. And he had learned them well. He knew what must be done and what could safely be done in progressing from arrest to conviction. He was aware of what words had to be spoken and what proof needed to be adduced at different times in order for his own activities to be legitimated —within both the police and the judicial bureaucracies.

Still, he had to make all sorts of choices. Simply facing someone about to swallow the evidence requires a selection among alternatives. In theory, an officer's duty was clear: risk injury, try to rescue the paper. But this John rejected out-of-hand as unpleasant, unsanitary, and because it was inconsistent with his own self-image, degrading. Most important, it was simply unnecessary in order for him to comfortably effect his own priorities.

Another version of duty would have John making the arrest even after the list had gone down. This would mean putting in the district attorney's lap a decision about whether or not to prosecute on scanty evidence—John's testimony alone—which would probably be insufficient for a conviction. According to unwritten rules of the bureaucracy, John could not make a practice of bringing these "questionable" cases in for the next labeling stage, conviction, without precipitating an embarrassing confrontation between, on the one hand, the law itself, through its rules of evidence, and, on the other, his and the DA's occupational concern with getting convictions. Since questionable cases served no one's convenience, they were tacitly considered unimportant compared to cases in which the evidence and its accompanying narrative were relatively problem-free. Any officer would be viewed as dense or peevish if he consistently failed to adapt to this simple operational norm of the bureaucracy.

It was, therefore, as a "pro" that John recognized only two options that could be considered seriously: to commit a crime that would salvage the contact's future—offering a working copy in exchange for surrender of the actual evidence—while assuring his arrest and conviction; or to commit a different crime—manufacturing evidence and a story to go with it—which John believed was less honorable. In the terms of John's and the system's priorities, both alternatives functioned to vindicate his activities, to make the time that he spent on the job worthwhile rather than wasted.

Since the alternatives met this essential criterion, ranking them in the order that he did appears eminently sensible. His preferred choice was more humane. It salvaged a man's pocketbook and offered at least some assurance that he would be able to get his old job back after his encounter with the law's bureaucracy. Moreover, it proved to John that he himself was trustworthy and not becoming unnecessarily harsh—in short, that he was still a decent fellow not a "rotten apple." John described himself to me in terms that he felt a layman would approve: he was not lazy; he was conscientious. He was willing to do his job in the "right way" so long as he *could* do it that way. He had, after all, to do something. Nor had he become cynical about human nature, unlike other officers he knew. Rather than just writing off the possibility that criminals would respond to human decency, John reaffirmed his humanistic faith even in them: before resorting to planting evidence, he always gave someone a chance to surrender his list "voluntarily." Thus, John's own plants, in cases that he wanted me to believe were "rare," could be justified because forced on him: "I only do it when I have to . . ."

The third alternative that was discussed was for John to merely walk away once the intended evidence became unavailable. Unless he actually saw the contents of a list before it was swallowed, this was, in fact, the only lawful one of the lot. And it was the alternative that was consistent with official police regulations. But while law might abstractly accept the notion that someone should not be arrested unless there is evidence against him, a policeman could not, in good conscience, take a similar view. The option of walking away was the only one that John considered wholly untenable. Obeying the law would sabotage his own position. The reason was simple: no one would ever hand over a list. John would get known, and swallowing would become the passport to his customers' immunity.

The success of his technique ultimately depended on his maintaining his reputation for being ready, willing, and able to commit whatever crime was "necessary" to do his job and make arrests. To stay in business, he had to remain "respected." Otherwise, he would be unable to meet his obligations and professional commitments. This was "the system."

A different cop once explained his own system for outwitting judges at the second level of involvement, the trial. "If you want to win," he said, meaning get a conviction, "answer the DA weak. Be just a little slow and vague in some places. The judge is going to think you've been gotten to, that you're trying to do the guy [the defendant] a favor. And he's going to convict, or get the jury to convict." The converse was also true. "If you come on strong, too perfect, the judge thinks something's wrong, that you're trying too hard, that there must be a reason you have a hard-on for this particular guy, something's fishy about the whole thing. So he's likely to let him off."

How the law is actually implemented is related to the roles that exist within the system and determined by expectations of and about those both officially and functionally a part of it. Professed goals have only a limited effect on how the system works. More influential are the ways that bureaucracies successfully merge the personal behavior of individual participants with the interests of organizational survival and expansion.

¶ FITTING INTO THE SYSTEM: LAWYERS

The law bureaucracy, besides having several component professions, is concerned with more than one kind of law. In addition to its criminal operation, it perpetuates certain procedures said to constitute "private," or civil, law.

To see how the system shapes a lawyer, we can consider the typical civil negligence case. A client—the customer—hires his attorney to perform one service: getting money. Almost always, the lawyer's fee is "contingent." This means it depends on a money award being given the client. The lawyer receives nothing for his efforts—even, in most cases, for his out-of-pocket expenses—unless and until the client gets paid for injuries, pain, suffering, and financial loss sustained because of the civil defendant's "negligence." Then he gets "a percentage."

Many scholarly articles are devoted to proving that a difference exists between civil negligence and criminal responsibility. For the most part, however, the reasoning only provides a theoretical rationalization and justification for the plain fact that a convicted person in a criminal case suffers different practical consequences than the one who has lost a civil suit. Whether the technical distinction between the notion of negligence and the idea of criminality is logically valid or wholly imaginary, these two concepts have remarkable practical similarities in terms of the moral outrage they engender. The basic point in this context is that whatever difference exists is normally blurred over in the courtroom.

Any lawyer presenting a client's negligence case to a judge or jury tries to paint the defendant as having been recklessly in the wrong. The more indignation against the defendant he can arouse in every juror's breast, the more likely he is to win his plaintiff's case "big." In making a sympathetic pitch, he describes the client as grievously wronged and seriously harmed. Beyond this, however, he tries to implant in the jury's mind the opinion that, somehow, this defendant is a bad person. His aim, of course, is to twist a law that is nominally designed to compensate injured plaintiffs into a means for punishing the defendant—financially.

Attorneys who specialize in representing defendants in civil cases use the reciprocal tactic. Their clients (customers) are described as reasonable men being forced to defend themselves against baseless charges brought by unscrupulous individuals seeking to hit the jury jackpot. Plaintiffs are always depicted by these lawyers as opportunistic and litigious, greedy for outrageous awards, or just capitalizing on the fact that it doesn't cost anything to sue. The strategic payoff comes when the judge or jury is convinced of the truth of these characterizations. They "throw the case (or the plaintiff) out of court." The violent image conjured up by this fairly common phrase may fairly be taken as an indication of the strength of feelings preceding the action.

Fundamentally, each side attempts to create an impression that the other is perverting the judicial process by using the system in order to get away with something. What is at stake is a battle for each juror's mind: the defendant's lawyer trying to engender a feeling that the plaintiff doesn't deserve to win, that he is the sort of person who lies, that he is manipulating the law rather than claiming his just due; the plaintiff's lawyer seeking to imbed in the jury's thinking the idea that the defendant has to be taught a lesson, that he is a threat and menace to social order as proven by his first injuring the plaintiff, and following up by now trying to hoodwink the jury.

A lawyer has two reasons for identifying with his client. The first of these is bread-and-butter. In the case of the plaintiff's attorney, he of course identifies his own fee with the amount of the client's recovery. He feels rejected, financially and personally, if the client gets nothing. For the defense counsel, financial identification with a client's cause is equally realistic. Although not retained on a reverse contingency (a percentage of what the suing plaintiff *didn't* win), the defense lawyer known for pulling difficult cases out of the fire gets more business and commands higher fees. No specific quota of defendants' verdicts is expected. But, informally, such a quota does exist, determined by averages and by what the competition can produce—or promise. When talking to a hard-nosed insurance executive, the defense lawyer cannot comfortably shrug off a string of expensive losses with the simple explanation that the plaintiffs had better cases than the defense. The inference to be drawn from these losses is inescapable: they also had better lawyers. The insurance executive will surely look at the latest scores of other defense firms.

On both sides, therefore, one reason lawyers identify with their clients has to do with their general standing and status within the profession, that is, income.

The second reason identification occurs is more complex. Ideological, moral, and psychological factors enter the picture. In the same way that a good actor *is* the part that he plays, a trial lawyer—whose job is very similar to an actor's —cannot fake his feelings for long and stay in business. Or, conversely, just staying in practice encourages identification, as one of his tricks of the trade. A grizzled defense lawyer once told me, in all sincerity, that he settled every case in which he felt that the plaintiff was telling the truth. "The trouble is," he said, "over ninety-nine percent of them are lying."

Since the trial lawyer's technique requires him constantly to villify the opposing client and reconstitute his own client's reputation—in both subtle and very direct ways—it would be a rare human being who could stand up to this job day in and day out without coming to believe that he is really on the side of the angels. One aspect of the trial lawyer's work requires him to sift through his opponent's evidence and testimony and seize upon flaws and contradictions, often on very short notice. From these he has to imply that the whole case is a put-up. By the same token, he has to guard against similar treatment from his adversary by seeking out in advance apparent inconsistencies in his own client's story, anticipating an attack, and rationalizing these contradictions into a fabric of perfect plausibility.

A lawyer, then, is occupationally oriented toward making negative generalizations and inferences about the opposing party while at all times zealously championing his own client's moral purity.

This situation contains certain parallels to what we have already encountered in our examination of the police in action. Like the cop, a lawyer's concern with winning is related to three factors: job security, the accomplishments of those in the same field with whom he is compared, and the need to give meaning and abstract significance to activities that he believes are uniquely characteristic of his field. Attaining what he wants in these areas necessitates his making harsh moral judgments about the other side in order to justify the trickery of his own professional activities.

The fact that both police and trial work are structured in an adversary setting means that the very existence of an "other" side sets up a target to be discredited and creates a "him-or-me" mentality. What has to be done in such a context is made palatable because the lawyer and the cop are able to place a moral and psychological distance between themselves and the other side. A process of "reverse identification" and disassociation occurs by which the practitioner merges his personality with the abstraction of Justice and "my job and duty." He fits into a ready-made schema of good-guys and bad-guys. Later we will consider the functional effect of these abstractions.

All of this is aided by the oversimplification and characterization required by the law. Right or wrong, did he or didn't he, guilty or innocent, find for the plaintiff or the defendant: these are the operational end-products of the system to which professionals within the law bureaucracy have to adjust their functioning.

¶ REGULATION AND SELF-REGULATION

The will to win may be common to all of us. But there is probably a factor of selection that causes certain jobs to appeal to people with a particularly high quotient of combativeness. Law and police work in particular attract individuals who can function by expressing aggressiveness within a protected setting. After they have received their commissions, opportunities for specialization (for example, in trial work) permit them to seek their own levels, where their particular characteristics and personality needs can be accommodated. Law and police work have in common the chance they give practitioners to act out pugilistic impulses in a socially approved arena, limited by certain special rules that are both written and implied.

So long as these impulses appear confined to this official arena and appear to have been conducted in accordance with the rules, the practitioner's professional standing confers on him virtually total immunity from the usual (nonprotected) consequences of such behavior.

In court, for example, a lawyer's defamatory comments are "privileged"—that is, he can say almost anything he wants about anybody. Only when he insults the judge or otherwise impugns the integrity of the legal system itself does he run into any danger of being bridled. Even then, a judge about to cite a lawyer for contempt thinks twice. Perhaps he is going to have to reckon with strong protests from a lawyers' lobby with the power to make his personal life uncomfortable and affect his reputation and future in a higher court. And aside from the fact that everyone has doubts about the accuracy with which he is drawing an imaginary line, a judge's own past training and experience as a lawyer make him sensitive to charges that he is stifling free speech, depriving clients of full representation, and tampering with the time-hallowed prerogatives of advocacy. For these reasons he is inclined to allow a lawyer's "privileged" status full rein except in cases where the lawyer's tactics are to provoke a confrontation intentionally, that is, to flaunt and break the special rules upon which his privilege rests.

Most of the forces that might check a lawyer's wide latitude of aggression exist, then, only on paper. These forces are themselves effectively limited by traditional interests within the legal system.

Similarly, relatively few constraints actually operate on enforcement components of the system. Those constraints that do exist are verbal, for the purpose of establishing "a record"—the appearance of limits—rather than actual control. For just as transactions between lawyer and client occur in the privacy of a law office, so most contacts between enforcers and their captive customers take place in secret, and there is little hope of monitoring either. Moreover, when presented with specific complaints by someone who claims to have been mishandled by the police, a judge and jury are being asked, in substance, to choose between the credibility of someone under a cloud of a criminal charge and one with all the perquisites and credentials of a duly appointed agent of respectable society. At stake is something more comprehensive than the particular conduct of one officer in a local situation. Accordingly, the verdict of judge and jury exonerates the officer, except in rare instances where the proof against him is inescapable.

In terms of the police force itself, when a cop is "caught," the prevailing attitude among his fellows is not that he went too far but that he had been clumsy and stupid enough not to cover his tracks. All attempts at control are governed by the interests of the force. Police behavior in New York City, for example, is regulated by the cops themselves (whose special unit to handle this task is nick-named the "shoe-fly" squad). Similarly, in early 1970, New York's mayor appointed a small investigation committee to look into graft, corruption, and police practices. Its members were all city officials—including the police and the investigations commissioners—whose existing jobs called for them to be doing just what the investigation itself was presumably going to do. More, it should have been plain enough that any findings of the committee would necessarily be neutralized by being screened through the grid of its own members' personal and professional stakes in the outcome. Still, the police immediately brandished a "sick-in" that threatened to paralyze the city's entire enforcement operation—until an accommodation was reached specifying that no "witch hunt" was going to ensue. This code phrase was a guarantee that, although a few heads might roll and perhaps some administrative changes be made, the system's overall functioning would not be imperilled. (This "you-can't-do-without-us-so-better-take-us-on-our-own-terms" weapon had already been successfully deployed a few years earlier when the police union beat a civilian review board at the polls. Apparently, city officials learned a lesson from the vote, having since then confined their efforts at reform to proposals that would be monitored by and from within the system.)

The arguments raised by lawyers and police to continue their freedom to do their own thing are parallel ones. Lawyers cite the imminence of a police state and the dangers of governmental over-regulation. Police trot out the argument that crime will become rampant if they are "shackled." These contentions are generally persuasive enough to prevent any changes, because of the spectre of extremism they raise. As a result, professional conduct—as it takes place in private—is generally unaffected by regulations, laws, and court decisions that are ostensibly designed to control conduct. Rather, these laws, regulations, and decisions serve to keep unacceptable conduct out of public sight and to avoid confrontations that would expose the gap between reality and professed norms. Such showdowns would suggest the need for more fundamental changes to align the norms with reality or vice-versa. The actual function of self-regulatory mechanisms is to maintain an appearance of external control while, for example, police review boards and bar association disciplinary committees continue to represent and assert the interests of the very professions that are apparently being regulated. The public's modest demands for occasional sacrificial victims impose a tolerable toll of appeasement, a cheap purchase price for stability and for the assurance of business more-or-less as usual.

¶ POST POSITIONS

"Shackling" the police means requiring their conformity to the stated law and to official rules of conduct and procedure. This, if it ever occurred, would result in a different balance, between the crimes of police and those of the citizens whom they hunt down, than the balance that currently exists. Conversely, giving the enforcement establishment greater leeway to disregard official rules—under a banner, say, of law and order—would definitely result in more arrests and convictions, just as hiring more cops would achieve this same result. But neither "shackling" nor "unleashing" can, by itself, affect the total amount of crime in a community. Rather, the existing balance between the two merely indicates whose crime is currently being tolerated.

The clashing prerogatives of defense and prosecution in a trial—of government *versus* the individual—may be considered to be either the same or reciprocal interests being asserted by opposing sides (for example, by cops and lawyers) within the system. Each side zealously guards the current distribution of prerogatives—and grabs for more. While fighting at least to maintain the status quo of power distribution, each also clamors for a balance that is more favorable to itself. This battle—for example, for easier burdens of proof, more lenient "presumptions" that may be inferred from the evidence, and for greater leeway for one side or the other in obtaining or excluding evidence or confessions —is triggered off by the knowledge that law decisions are predetermined by a trial's legally permissible input.

The preparation, development, and presentation of a case is wholly oriented toward outcome—with the power of different professions (as well as the weal of individual practitioners) always at stake behind the scenes. Each separate component of the law bureaucracy evolves norms and operational procedures that it considers essential for the maintenance of its own status. These become translated into the idiom of the law system's ideology—that is, Justice. An example of this process in action was John's rationalization of his activities on the basis of his victims' "guilt."

Reasoning of this sort is then amplified in order to identify whatever activities they are supposed to justify with the survival of the whole legal and social system. Thus, John implied that his conduct was necessary in order for the police to continue functioning, an approach that was intended to strike a sympathetic and responsive chord among fellow professionals who must also work the system. As a lawyer, I was expected to appreciate the common denominator that John was conjuring up.

¶ JOCKEYING

While John was offering his self-image of the enforcement professional in action, he and I were acting out another kind of relationship, one that exemplifies transactions that take place between different professions within the same system.

From an examination of this overlap and of what went on between us in our respective professional capacities, it will be possible to learn about inter-professional transactions that involve lawyers and others—including the police—in civil cases. This will shed light on exactly what constitutes a lawyer's profession and clarify his particular role and function in the bureaucracy.

In its general outlines, my behavior was fairly typical of what occurs at the lawyer's end of the business. I wanted my client to survive not just for humanitarian reasons but also so that he would be able to testify at the trial. At the end of my activities, I expected a financial return commensurate with the considerable time, money, and emotional energy that had been invested in the case. This investment, by itself, became the secret yardstick by which the case value was measured, replacing many other factors, intrinsic to the case itself, by which a lawyer initially evaluates the "worth" of his client's cause and determines his investment.

Rightly or wrongly, I attributed to my opponent the converse hope that the client would be stricken before trial and the case, therefore, dismissed, projecting that he was engaged in certain illegal, behind-the-scenes manipulations of the calendar for the purpose, and with the effect, of causing uncertainty about when we were going to select a jury. In these projections, I was making psychological preparation for transferring my attitude about the other lawyer from him to his client (the ultimate wrong-doer!) by the time we got to trial. My earlier doubts about which driver had actually passed the red light were forgotten and, in the interests of Justice I had now no recourse but to fight fire with fire—just as John had to fight fire with fire when faced with a bookie about to swallow his list.

For five days I answered the call of the calendar by saying that the case was actually ready for trial, knowing that the client was three hours away in another state and planning, if necessary, to take as much of the judge's and jurors' time as possible before admitting that he wasn't even in court. To accomplish this, I had gone about seducing John to my own purposes. He was the only possible fill-in whose testimony could precede the client's.

I was willing to make veiled references to reimbursement, use whatever charm could be mustered over coffee, and adopt any apparent attitude toward the police that he might require. While John was enjoying these daily interludes away from work, we both knew the city was being cheated of his services and that, properly, I should arrange the impossible: to summon him from the precinct an hour before he was to take the stand. What I was doing—intentionally, in order to win the case—was making sure that John would not be what he and I were going to pretend to the jury that he was: objective, disinterested in the outcome, simply a cop who had been ordered to an accident as part of his official duties. With whatever limited psychological resources were available in this situation, I was hoping to transform him into my client's safe witness, emotionally an advocate himself, indignant at the defendant, sympathetic to the plaintiff—both of whom he had seen only briefly once before. I was brainwashing him for a "favorable" response to possible questions on cross examination dealing, for example, with the accuracy of his present memory about an event that had occurred five years earlier. Unless he, too, could be enticed into having an investment in the case, for whatever reasons and by any means, he would be incapable of being wary of the defense lawyer's cross examination traps. He simply wouldn't care.

5

LAWYERS AND CLIENTS:
WHO CONTROLS WHOM?

A POLITICAL science student at Yale recently wrote his doctoral thesis on the subject of lawyer-client relationships in negligence cases. The chapter dealing with his methodology begins by describing what he first hoped to accomplish and continues with an account of how he was finally forced, in his own way, to "settle." His sinuous odyssey itself resembles some of the experiences typically encountered by young lawyers trying to settle their first negligence case with an insurance company claims adjuster. At every turn the novice is hopelessly outmaneuvered, but then he wheels, undaunted, and tries a new tack. This aside, the dissertation narrative is unsurpassed as a documentation of the fate that invariably befalls those who try to part the curtains of secrecy draping a lawyer's inner sanctum.

It begins with an academically reasoned battle plan that fairly takes into account everyone's interests:

> I approached 18 experienced lawyers with the following proposal: I would be present during one or more consultations they would conduct with two or three of their clients . . . who would be apprised of the research and . . . free to decline involvement. . . . These observations would be kept in strict confidence and the final draft of the manuscript would be submitted to each attorney to assure his own and his client's anonymity.

But suddenly the researcher is hit with the old one-two:

> Politely, all refused. . . . First, my presence during an actual consultation . . . might jeopardize the confidential nature of the client's statements to his attorney. . . . The second reason given for the attorneys' refusals was even the request to participate would be an imposition upon their clients; they were unwilling to risk incurring their clients' displeasure by the mere invitation to participate in such a research inquiry.

Thrown off-balance, Dink Stover ruminates on his lack of success:

> I sensed that two other considerations were involved in their refusals. There was "nothing in it" for the lawyers to cooperate with me. Why should they expose themselves to what would be at best an inconvenience and at worst a serious disruption? . . . Furthermore, lawyers are not used to having people—even colleagues—look over their shoulder when they talk to clients. The presence of an outside observer would put them on the spot and might lead to disquieting findings about their desk-side manner.

He feints:

All of these objections applied with equal force to the idea of taping actual consultations with no observer present. This variation had been explored by Harrop Freeman and abandoned when he met with lawyer resistance.

Then he adduces another plan—which is, however, not quite artful:

> I next thought of simulated interaction between real lawyers and people posing as clients, but this raised formidable and personally uninteresting tactical problems of experimental design. . . .

Besides, an honest assessment of his prowess rules it out:

> Simulation requires either a rigorous and explicit theory or detailed knowledge about the subject under investigation. . . . I didn't know enough.

He is in a corner:

> The next best data source after direct observation is interviews with lawyers and clients about what went on during their interaction involving recently terminated legal problems. . . .

Still more blows rain down:

> Even this modification was met with reluctance by the same 18 lawyers, apparently for the two generally unarticulated reasons already indicated.

He finds himself on the ropes, the clock ticking away:

> I soon realized that the only way to get meaningful information and on with the inquiry was to go to clients directly rather than to lawyer intermediaries.

And at last he climbs down from the ring:

> After four fruitless months, this was the approach I adopted.

Not only in negligence but in every kind of law, from corporate to matrimonial litigation, it is hard enough to describe the essence of a lawyer's work and to get to the bottom of his relationship with the client.

One mistake commonly made in analyzing this relationship is assuming that the client has less at stake than the lawyer and therefore can afford to be more honest and objective in reporting what transpires in the inner sanctum. According to this reasoning, the client is at least accessible, constrained only by whether or not he might be criticized for revealing the substance of certain privy transactions such as, for example, his business secrets. As the Yale student wrote in his thesis, "Interviewers find that . . . people usually like to be interviewed." It is, however, a big jump to equate access with validity.

The truth of the matter is that a client's picture of his lawyer at work is inherently suspect—not just because of the client's ignorance of whatever legal technicalities have been involved but because the client is, and feels, thoroughly implicated in the lawyer's doings. He confers with his lawyer either to find out what has to be done in order to get what he wants or, somehow, to impart to his lawyer the urgency of doing whatever is necessary to gain this end. Long before the initial interview, the client has concluded that he is "right" and "deserves" to win or to get whatever he is after. Usually, he comes to this conclusion for reasons having nothing to do with the legal "merits" of his case. These are just the rules within which he thinks a lawyer operates and within which he will be justified. *His* decision

meanwhile has arisen out of whatever set of rules he believes in, and the client is at the lawyer's office only because
his goal must be effected through the manipulation of law,
society's set of rules. In ten years, I have been approached
only once by a client who said: "I want to bring on this suit
just because the law says I can win." No defendant sees a
lawyer in order to tell him: "I did it. The law says I should
pay. Therefore, I want to pay. Go in there and see that I
do." The law is seldom the heart of the matter for clients.

It is this background that results in the clients' belief that
essentially a partnership characterizes the lawyer-client relationship. In the final analysis, most clients feel that they
have either set or joined in setting the fundamental tone of
their case. This is especially true for those who acquiesce in
a lawyer's "leave-everything-to-me" approach because they
feel most assured that the lawyer understands the nature of
their concern.

In describing transactions with a lawyer, then, a client's
narration is likely to emerge as a projection of his own role
and wishes, an inversion or at least a confusion of responsibilities. For example, every lawyer has had the experience
of a client switching to or away from him during a case.
Whether corporate or an individual, the client invariably ac-
cuses the culprit attorney of "not doing enough," of being
too passive or negligent to get the desired results. Another
favorite imputation is that the erstwhile lawyer was bought
off by the other side. These attacks reflect the client's obses-
sion with getting favorable results. Actually, he is rarely in a
position to judge, even if he knows, the steps that were
taken on his behalf. What the client is doing when discussing his case with the lawyer is merely transmitting signals about his own desires and demanding some spurt of
legal activity that will seem responsive to them. If one law-

yer doesn't seem to get the message, another gets the case.

In an ongoing relationship between a particular client and his lawyer—say, the corporate officer with "house counsel" or with an "outside" lawyer to whom he regularly refers the company's legal work—a pattern of expectations has usually been established. The very fact that there is an accumulated residue of understanding that carries over from one case to the next reduces the amount of explicit communication that needs to take place. The important interactions may be expressed in verbal shorthand, code words, or, simply, as an implicit understanding about the circumstances and imperatives that draw the two together in their unique relationship. Each side takes certain cues from the other. If these nuances were put into language, the dialogue would go something like this:

CLIENT: Here's what I want. Get it done. Call me in as little as you have to but, still, make sure I know about any risks that you might not overcome. You're navigator, but I'm the captain. On your information and advice I may decide to change destinations. But a good navigator should get us there with only course corrections.

LAWYER: It's in my hands now. From time to time I'm going to need information and your cooperation. I'll transmit warning signals that indicate where you better trim here and there, how to interpret this and construe that. Together we'll avoid the shoals and get you where you want to go.

In the one-time relationship, this situation is only slightly different. The same demand and the same commitment are still implied. Although a lawyer is less dependent on any one non-repeater client, he has to make up for not being on a payroll by getting a steady volume of cases from many separate sources. The result is a sort of co-captaincy in each case. Having waited in the marketplace—according to the canons of ethics, passively—to get chartered as ship's pilot, the lawyer is as much concerned about destination as is his client. This is particularly true when his financial reward depends in whole or part on safe passage.

Although he has to seem willing to go almost anyplace, within limits, the implied assurances that he gives at the beginning of the relationship amount, essentially, to business "puffing." Once the recruitment stage is past and he is actually hired, however, a lawyer has to contend with limitations imposed by his own abilities and the reach of his contacts, with the realities of certain unalterable facts about the case itself, and, above all, with the desirability of preserving his client as a possible source of future business or referrals.

Chief among the factors that increase the pressure on lawyers to assume control and call the shots is that it is only a matter of time before the potential conflict between every lawyer's and every client's interest blossoms into the open. These conflicts are of various sorts. In general, the lawyer can resolve a conflict to his own advantage by acting decisively. The nature of the conflict—which can express itself in either ideological or financial terms—and of the case determine his options and how they will be exercised. This may mean prolonging, curtailing, trying, settling, or appealing a case; it may mean taking a hard line or a flexible one with the other side; it may mean extending conferences behind the scenes or taking a case to the forum of public opinion. We shall examine some typical conflicts in order to explore their relationship to the lawyer's options.

By waiting for a trial, a client in an accident case may ultimately get more money than he would if the case were settled early. But completing trial preparations requires a lawyer to spend time and money. Therefore, despite a possibly larger gross fee if the case is tried, he may end up with the same profit or even in the red. Then, too, he may face an unappreciative client who feels the award that he waited for so long was too low—primarily, in his judgment, because of his lawyer's inept courtroom performance. Knowing these possibilities, a lawyer may realistically decide that it is in his own interest to dispose of a case at the first chance of settlement, despite the fact that the client's bread is buttered on the side of trial or, at least, seems to be.

When a lawyer's fee is not contingent, few clients are willing to pay the "fair" value of legal work without considering the optimal value of their case. Even the exception proves the rule: in the rare instance where a well-heeled client is proceeding "on a matter of principle," there is still a limit to how long he will keep paying for legal work, without seeing any tangible results, before he reacts with the cry or feeling that the lawyer is milking him. From the client's viewpoint, there must always be some profitable relationship between his legal costs and his risk of loss or chance of gain. This yield may only be in the form of advertising or "insurance," as when a corporation pays more in legal fees than would be required to settle the claim so as to discourage a welter of similar suits in the future and to maintain its image of official correctness and integrity. Sometimes these same considerations may dictate the opposite course. But the yield must be there. Normally, the first question a client asks, when quoted the lawyer's straight hourly rate, is: "How long will you have to work on it?" Next, he wants the lawyer's estimate of his approximate "chances."

Similarly, the lawyer looks upon every case as an income-producing package. He may not think only of money. What has been called "psychic income" can be defined in this instance in terms of the lawyer's personal and professional values. He may place premiums on headlines, hobnobbing, being in a high court, repaying favors, getting an "in" with certain people, or a reputation in particular fields, seeking a judgeship and other political advantages, or advancing what he considers a worthwhile social "cause." These are but a few well-known factors that affect different individuals and determine the lawyer's willingness to stick with a particular case. But once he has evaluated the case potential in regard to all such factors (and of course money), he automatically places a ceiling on the investment that he can make in that particular case. This estimate can be revised from time to time, either upward or downward, and often is—sometimes resulting in client complaints such as those previously mentioned.

In assessing the potential of a case, the lawyer is concerned primarily with identifying his own priorities. There will be very little, and only accidental, overlap with the client's interests. The latter's sense of urgency has to do with considerations such as keeping out of jail, not being evicted, cutting through the bureaucracy of a municipal agency, marrying the "other woman," getting paid for a car crash, or completing a corporate acquisition; the former's with the factors of his professional career or personal satisfaction. Usually, these discrepancies become a matter of money.

A conflict of interest—and financial disagreement— between lawyer and client can be ruled out of their relationship in only two situations: in the rare instance in which the client is willing to pay for whatever the lawyer may come to think requires doing, no questions asked and regardless of the intrinsic value of the case (and both parties are aware of this arrangement at the outset); and when there happens to be an overlap between the lawyer's and the client's interest —say, the lawyer believes it worthwhile to take a financial loss in order to cement his relationship with the client, or the corporate house counsel is bucking for the position of corporate secretary, or the lawyer believes there is a pot of gold at the end of the case.

In all other instances, the lawyer must manipulate the tools of his trade so as to "break even" or get what he considers a fair profit.

Generally he aims to do this in one of three ways. The first and most comfortable is to quote a figure that is not necessarily the "going fee"—the greatest determinant of flat rates—but that allows him financial elbow room for those contingencies that actually arise. It is rare, though, that he obtains agreement on such an adequate fee in advance because the client senses that he is being overcharged. A second alternative, going back and renegotiating the fee as the case progresses, would be the most reasonable but is almost guaranteed to provoke the client into claiming either that he is being swindled or that his lawyer is incompetent.

The third manipulative alternative is the one most commonly used. The lawyer simply does those things in a case that he can afford to do. Then, somehow, he brings it to a close. This is not as difficult as it seems because usually at the other end there is a lawyer in that same boat with *his* client. If the two do not have approximately similar investments in their respective cases, there still inevitably comes a time when both reach the end of their tether. This difference in lawyer investments is then reflected in the terms of settlement—whether the case is a criminal or a civil one. Conversely, the terms of settlement normally reflect the relative power positions, in regard to the case, of the lawyers on each side—their risks, past investments, and their estimates of what future investments might be required in order to alter materially the balance of power between them. In short, most cases end when the lawyers are strategically played out in terms of the investments they have made and feel they can afford—that is, according to their final positions on the playing board.

In order to pull off making a living in this fashion, it is necessary that the lawyer have authority over his client. When a negligence case is being settled on the phone, for example, it is not uncommon for the adjuster or insurance attorney to ask the plaintiff's lawyer: "Do you control your client?" This is frequently an acknowledgment that the settlement being accepted is on the low side. (Of course, the lawyer has previously sought the highest figure he thinks can be pried out of the company without his having to over-invest in the case.) At the point of telephone settlement, the adjuster would "look bad" if he marked his file as settled only to learn later that the plaintiff himself rejected the offer that the lawyer had accepted. If the lawyer does not categorically assure him that the case is closed, then, the adjuster either makes no memorandum of the conversation or a false one, stating his true offer but a fictitious higher demand by the plaintiff's lawyer. He then waits until the lawyer calls back to say that the figure has been okayed by the client.

There is a standard way to get this clearance. The lawyer calls the client and announces that he has been successful in obtaining an offer from the insurance company. But, he explains, notwithstanding the long wait to trial and perils that might result in the plaintiff's getting nothing, he would recommend rejecting the offer. He then mentions the amount of the offer—setting it lower than the true figure already approved by the insurer. He goes on to say that the "best advice" he can give the client at this point is to sit tight and take his chances on trial—adding, however, that he plans on making one final try with the company. He recommends that the client consider accepting another figure, one higher than the amount he has named but still lower than the actual offer.

By now, the client is usually in despair at seeing any money from the case, convinced that the lawyer is, if anything, too much on his side. He feels caught between an offer he is told not to accept and a trial he is told he will probably lose. Whatever figure the lawyer said would be "fair"—which is, of course, still less than the figure the lawyer already had up his sleeve—the client readily agrees to accept. Appending a few more words about not being optimistic, the lawyer then hangs up, calls back the adjuster, and confirms the original offer. A few days later he breaks the good news to the client—who gratefully signs settlement papers and release forms, no questions asked.

A similar appeal to the lawyer's self-interest in limiting his investment—an interest that has long ago parted company with the client's—is often made by the judge himself, in chambers, during last-ditch efforts to save the time and expense of trial. It is not uncommon for him to sit down with the plaintiff's lawyer and map out in black and white the difference in fee between the offered amount and that which the lawyer is claiming would be reasonable for a jury to award. The judge divides this difference by the number of days the trial will be likely to last, points out legal pitfalls in the plaintiff's case that create the possibility that he will lose altogether, and then asks the lawyer if it is "worth" taking the chance. This also implies that he is sure the lawyer can be earning much more back at his office doing other things—a flattering assumption that most would find demeaning to deny outright. Once the lawyer sees the light of this bird-in-the-hand reasoning, the judge points him toward the courtroom, where the client has been waiting apprehensively, and says, "Go outside and talk it over."

From the client's viewpoint things look rather differently.

If the lawyer has to control his client, we have also seen that the very existence of a professional relationship depends on the client believing that *he* is controlling *the lawyer*. He has to be convinced that his concerns have been communicated with such thoroughness that they have been adopted as the lawyer's own. The client's *belief* that he has accomplished this goal of communication is not incompatible with the lawyer's *actual* control over him. The reason for this is that the client can only reassure himself. He has to proceed without objective proof. Usually, his touchstone is whether or not he feels some rapport with the lawyer. Or he may ask himself whether the lawyer has what the client thinks it takes—aggressiveness, toughness, materialism, sympathy, intelligence, glibness, or contacts—for the kind of battle he envisions and the sort of victory he imagines. He also makes an estimate about the extent to which he has successfully primed the lawyer with zeal. These conclusions, however, are not really verifiable.

The client's is a world of hopes, of belief, seeming, feeling, imagining, and envisioning. He needs merely to be satisfied. His screening processes take place entirely in his own mind. Between the beginning and end of actual law work, he is pretty much removed from the picture and when, from time to time, he inquires or is called in to participate at disjointed stages in the career of his case, his opinion can again be formed only on the basis of appearances and speculation. Since he is both unaware of the real nature of the transactions that (may) have taken place in the interim and unqualified to judge them, even the outcome of his case cannot vindicate his evaluations.

The client acts as the first advocate for his case—with his own lawyer. Operating in a world of faith, he has to imply that his goal can be reached. This he does by overstating its reasonableness. He knows—or at least senses—that the lawyer cannot share his priorities because the lawyer's livelihood is made up of files and files of other people's urgent problems. Suspecting that the minute he leaves the office the lawyer is going to downgrade his goal or, at least, shift into low gear, the client tries to compensate for this anticipated slippage in advance.

During the preliminary exchanges, the lawyer must undertake contradictory tasks. He wants to keep up the client's spirits if the case is worth handling. But he must also dampen these spirits in order not to sabotage a probable compromise ending. Ideally, a satisfactory conclusion will ultimately be made to seem his legal miracle and an unsatisfactory one will appear at least acceptable. He must try to keep all doors open until able to form an opinion about what is really possible in the case given those things that he knows actually operate in law. He has to decide what sort of an investment can be made in it, how much work he can afford to do.

Little occurs during these preliminaries between client and lawyer, then, except mutual put-ons and the trading of a certain amount of information. Yet this is a critical stage. It forms the basis for a client's hunches about whether his lawyer has been sufficiently "switched on" to his cause. And for the lawyer, this point in the case is when he must stake his claim. Thereafter, he deals mostly with witnesses and professionals within the bureaucracy. Now he must sell effectively, utilizing some style that is going to cool the client. His immediate task is to close the deal.

It is not invariably a simple matter to learn what the client really wants. The lawyer may have to second-guess. People aren't always clear even to themselves about their own goals and, in other situations, cannot admit them. Sometimes they are simply not ready to act, and at other times it is actually the relationship between lawyer and client rather than a legal end-result that is most important to the client. Every lawyer, for example, has been consulted about an imminent divorce, only to have the client drop out of sight, then reappear again, a few years later, wanting urgently to proceed.

An extreme example is the case of Betty, a woman who came into my office apparently choked with rage and sorrow because her husband had moved out and was now, allegedly, having the proverbial affair with his secretary. After twenty-seven years of marriage, this was hard to take: "I've been so loyal," she said.

A lawyer ordinarily solves his problem of sorting out provables from legal fantasy by asking the client for examples. With Betty, however, these were not forthcoming. She just "knew" the affair was in progress. But since she had been existing for twenty-seven years on a modest allowance and no more wildly than was possible with a couple of Miami Beach and Catskill vacations, her present characterization of her husband—"not your ordinary plumber but a big contractor, a hidden millionaire"—didn't ring true. She knew of no bank accounts or other assets besides his medium-sized business. Still, his stored pot of gold was evidenced, to her, by the fact that "he always had money to throw around, cash . . . a tipper. . . ." Betty was sure, for example, that, somewhere behind an elaborate corporate veil, her mate owned the apartment building in which he presently occupied a single room—as, she explained, "a front."

After another conference I decided that she was just an ordinary Bronx matron with a history, until now, of only the usual marital snags. As for proving the alleged affair, I suggested that Betty hire an investigator. "No, no," she snapped. "Never again." It turned out that her stop before the lawyer's had been a detective's office. This man conducted surveillance during three weeks of what must have been the most innocent and frugal period of her husband's life—if the detective's written report, which Betty eventually produced, was to be reconciled with her husband's resources as she perceived them to exist. Betty's analysis of the disparity was different: the detective had "sold out" to her husband.

As she recounted stories that dubiously established her husband's habit of buying out such persons as building inspectors and revenue agents, Betty herself became very furtive. I asked what she was hiding. After considerable evasion, she finally blurted out that, while the detective was tailing her husband for proof of infidelity, he was also having an affair with her. "At first he seduced me. I think it was my husband who paid him to do it. So now I can never go into court," she said, bursting into tears. "He's a *rat!* To do this, *now* . . . ! Here, look!" She fished out of her pocketbook some tissues and a small, profile snapshot. It depicted a man in shirtsleeves, whose tongue was extended and actually making contact with the tip of his nose. "That's one of my husband's favorite tricks," she said, wiping her eyes.

It turned out that Betty, of course, didn't really want to go to court. In fact, when this was suggested as the only step likely to determine her financial rights, she instructed us to wait awhile. What Betty really wanted wasn't entirely clear: sympathy, therapy, or just a more meaningful menopause. Or, perhaps, she wanted to get even, to get her husband back or at least interested again—though she was making considerable of the real or imagined role of the wronged woman. Whatever her goal, she was indefatigable in search of it. Two or three weeks later, I got a call from another lawyer, who introduced himself, said he had been consulted and retained by Betty and would henceforth represent her in all dealings with her husband. As is customary, he asked that he be sent whatever legal matter in the file might be of use to him. I promptly forwarded a copy of my notes.

For all its oddities, this case is not unrepresentative. It indicates how easily the law can become a forum reflecting facets of the ambivalences and uncertainties that characterize personal relationships. Sometimes a lawyer is used for legal ends, sometimes he provides, essentially, a placebo effect. And the client's motivations, however varied, are often projected onto the lawyer—who may be asked to be brave, conciliating, aggressive, or loving, but who necessarily puts to himself quite other demands.

For all these reasons, a client's assessment of how the case was handled is primarily a derived measure of his own devotion to what he perceives as his goals.

6

THE BALANCE
OF ILLEGALITY

7. Describe briefly your associations with the applicant,
   setting forth how such associations began, and indicate
   in what activities (business, scholastic, cultural, recrea-
   tional, athletic, social or otherwise) you have participated with applicant. It is not sufficient answer merely
   to repeat the above words in parenthesis, but the *particular activities* should be specified.

8. How often during each week, month or year, or other
   division of time have you come in contact with applicant during the entire period of acquaintance or desig-
   nated parts thereof? ("Frequently" or "often" or other
   indefinite statement is not a satisfactory answer.)

9. What is your conclusion as to applicant's moral character? (Reserve details for next question.)

10. Set forth in *detail* what you have *personally observed* in
    your associations with applicant which leads you to the
    conclusion set forth under question 9, specifying, among

other things, the *moral* qualities and personal traits observed in applicant's conduct, and his usual attitude toward those with whom he associates.

14. (a) With what persons has the applicant lived during each period of your association with him in his home? (If during period or periods covered by answer, applicant has lived with family, enumerate the members of the family during each period. If, during any period of association, he has lived apart from his family, enumerate the persons, if any, with whom he has lived during each such period.)

(b) With what persons does he live at the present time, if that be known to you?

15. Set forth in *detail* what you have *personally observed* as to the *moral* qualities and conduct of the members of applicant's *family* or other persons with whom he has lived:

(a) in parental home;

(b) in marital home, if any;

(c) in any other home or place of abode applicant may have had.

16. What do you say of applicant's conduct toward the members of his family or household during each period of your association with him in his home, and at present, if association still continues? (Give full details.)

17. State fully any other facts within your knowledge, or of which you have information, which, in your opinion, have any bearing on the applicant's moral character or fitness to practice law, or which would be helpful to the Committee in determining the applicant's character and fitness.

—From "Affidavit of Character and Home Life," required in the Supreme Court, Appellate Division, Second Department, New York, for admission to the New York Bar.

From the scene of the accident the client had been taken by ambulance to the nearest hospital emergency room. After his release a few hours later, he was driven home and seen by his family physician, a Dr. Bell. He continued to be treated by Bell over the next several months, then moved to a different area. When his symptoms recurred sometime later, he consulted a doctor near his new home. While still under the care of this second physician, the client experienced sudden, serious complications and had to be hospitalized. Discharged a few weeks later, he began out-patient treatment at the hospital, which continued for the next half-year.

Dr. Bell was the link-pin. As the first doctor in the case, his testimony would be critical in proving that all of the client's subsequent medical woes were related to the same event—which was caused by the defendant.

A few weeks before this case was to be tried, and several years after the accident, I telephoned Dr. Bell. We arranged for a conference to review his records and discuss the testimony that he would give. After the call, I mailed him a copy of the same letter he had sent me several years before, which stated that its contents had been abstracted from his treatment notes. This letter reported the major outlines of my client's treatment and set forth Dr. Bell's medical opinions about the injuries. It was now an integral part of the case: by law, a doctor's report is sent to the lawyers for the defendant and a copy is also filed in court.

Dr. Bell had a thriving family practice. I waited in his anteroom until the last of an assorted variety of patients left, then introduced myself. As we shook hands, he gave a startling wink, without a smile, and invited me into his study behind one of the examining rooms.

"That report," he said. "I think the patient's wife may

have dictated or typed it. But don't worry, counselor," he added, reassuringly. "I've got some records here. We're all set." Again, the wink.

Dr. Bell sat down and started riffling through a mound of papers on his desk—rather purposelessly, I thought. "Yes . . . Smith . . . bad crackup . . . a nice guy . . ." he murmured. Then, to me, "Big case, eh?" Before I had a chance to answer, he continued to himself: ". . . didn't think much of the wife . . . alcoholic. . . ." Abruptly he drew out a sheaf of large-sized index cards. "Aha!" Now, crisply, "Here we are, counselor. Of course," he said, brandishing them fan-shaped, like out-sized playing cards, "you need *my* testimony, don't you?" I readily agreed. Once more he winked, from behind his winning hand, and this time I tried a smile. "Take a look at these," he said. "See if there's anything else you want me to add. But I think you'll find I did my homework."

He handed over the cards ceremoniously. They were supposed to be his contemporaneous treatment records. Obviously, however, they were not five years old. They were, in fact, new. But he had taken care to vary the pens used for each entry. While I was reading he said, proudly, "I guess we hit all of the treatment dates that were on that report you sent me, didn't we?"

His "treatment records" conformed closely to the report. Occasional frills and flights of medical fancy made it seem all the more as if he actually had used them to prepare the report. Putting the bogus records aside, I discussed the grounds that I expected to cover on direct examination, likely areas of cross examination, his fee for testifying (extremely reasonable, as these things go), and the days and hours that he would be available for court.

After about twenty minutes, I got up to leave. Dr. Bell

took his treatment records from the desk. As I moved toward the door, he suddenly lunged ahead of me and began vigorously rubbing each card up and down against the wall. Watching this performance, I no doubt looked very surprised. "*That* ought to make the damn things look old," he grunted, continuing to rub and scrape. I dredged up something not very funny about "doctoring" the records. He gave me a wink and, this time, smiled.

"Tell me what I have to say. She says I'm supposed to have overheard some conversations. One time before the wedding he is supposed to have said he wanted children and, another time afterwards, that he never wanted them but had just said that to get her to marry him. Basically, I know he doesn't like kids. So it's not that far from the truth. So I'll be your witness and say whatever I have to say."

"Look, if it'll help you out, I'll be glad to say he was here with me all the time. Nobody could ever prove different. I like the bastard, no matter what he did. Besides, the cops are just down on him."

I had been flown to Arizona for the conference. Now we were sitting in a cocktail lounge on the top floor of a hotel. "Here's the thing," said the organization man, pausing over his martini. "Every year or so we have a New York case. From now on you'll handle them all. Charge whatever you want for yourself and then figure me in. I want one-fifth back in cash. You have to declare taxes on my share, so figure them in, too. That'll be our arrangement. Okay?" His voice suddenly lowered. "How'd you like a piece of *that* action . . . ?" His eyes wandered all over the young thing being tucked into a nearby chair by her escort. Then he stroked his glass.

One day, coming home from work, I was stopped by a neighbor who asked if I minded giving him a "legal opinion." He spoke in confidential tones, explaining that his wife had been in a car accident some months ago and their lawyer had just sent them a letter saying he had now "succeeded in settling the case."

"What I want to know," he said, "is whether $1250 is a good settlement for a $200 medical bill."

I said it was, knowing that his wife hadn't seemed incapacitated at any time in the recent past.

"Of course, the lawyer gets almost half. Not that I'm complaining," he added. "I can see the lawyer deserves it. But that only leaves us with just about $450, because— do you know what?—that stinking doctor he sent us to really expects his $200 and she *actually* saw him only once!"

Any lawyer willing to speak frankly can etch a hundred similar vignettes from the stuff of his practice. This sampling is not presented in order to pass judgment on the modern sort of Robin Hood morality it reflects but to illustrate the network of expectations that converge on a lawyer because of his role within the bureaucracy of the law.

Every day he is deluged with propositions, some presented expressly and others through unmistakable inference. Even if he isn't going to avail his client of them, he is considered a safe repository for these offers, bound to secrecy by some form of legal *omerta*, the Mafioso's oath of silence. Usually, he becomes subtly implicated, even at the offering stage, because of his personal stake and accepted investment in the client's cause. As a well-known civil rights attorney recently stated to a gathering of law students at New York University: "If you're not corrupt, you're a loser."

In its most simple form, this assessment is illustrated by the man who offered to perjure himself in a divorce case. He just tells the lawyer that he's willing to become "your witness." Dr. Bell's approach was more oblique. First, he confirmed that he was indispensable to the case. Then he cemented my involvement by means of a pantomime that assured him I was in on the scheme of his faked records. Without lying outright—which, short of an official investigation, he could discount in the case of a fellow "professional" —I wouldn't later be able to deny having known or pretend that I had missed any of his earlier, more subtle, signals. Only then was he free to smile. By taking the initiative in putting himself out on a limb, ostensibly for my own and the patient-client's sake combined, he insulated himself from being requested to testify just from the report that he had sent and without any records. Although technically admissible, this testimony would be very unpleasant because of the rugged cross examination that would be inevitable. The opposing lawyer would surely make hay by portraying the doctor as a quack for having kept no records of his supposedly extensive treatment or a liar for claiming to have lost them. The doctor also knew that I would have to consider that the case would fall apart if he were discredited on the witness stand or simply refused to testify in the first place. Medically unexplained gaps between the accident and the onset of symptoms might make it impossible to prove that the client's injuries had anything to do with the accident. By offering to let me add anything I wanted to the "records," he was presenting me with an opportunity to overcome this problem in spades if I played the game his way. The reasonableness of his fee was just more icing on the cake.

All of the above illustrations have in common that they involve those with far less of a stake than clients in the outcome of a case. In fact, these people need not have gotten involved at all. Their interests were peripheral—like the doctor's in his patient's winning—or derivative—like the proposed alibi witness in the criminal case who announced that, by offering to lie, he was primarily expressing resentment of the police. In varying degrees, money, personal loyalty, reputation, convenience, and feelings about the establishment and its official norms account for all these offers of voluntary self-incrimination. But such offers, coming from those widely separated on and representative of the social spectrum, also demonstrate what might be called a balance of illegality.

Since the individuals involved did not have the distorted motivations that usually accompany a desire to win one's own case and could not be readily identified with any "criminal fringe," one might be tempted to write off a large part of society as just plain corrupt or to assume that things would be rosy if only lawyers had more backbone. But these notions are appealing oversimplifications. They bypass the more challenging concept that laws are never intended to be administered evenly but rather reflect what is actually done by some and cannot appear to be done by all without seeming to threaten the existing social order—that they constitute, in a manner of speaking, a balance of illegality. "Illegal" behavior, in this perspective, is made up of activities that have been legislatively identified as *socially desired if confined within certain bounds, practiced by certain people or groups, and carried on under conditions of limited visibil-*

ity or with acceptable moral rationalizations. There is no need to outlaw something that nobody does or wants to do. Thus, to qualify as illegal, an activity must be proven socially tempting by its actually being, or likely becoming, widespread. Furthermore, the activity must be seen as potentially dangerous, that is, interfering with existing customs if practiced beyond the confines that have been (more or less arbitrarily) assigned. There is no need to outlaw an activity that everyone can do without disturbing the apparent status quo.

This idea of a balance of illegality can be illustrated by an event that took place in a county contiguous to New York City. Police were getting nowhere in their negotiations for increased pay and easier working conditions. They rejected the tactic of a strike, which would have been "illegal," and instead instituted an enforcement crackdown. Every day, hundreds of motorists received tickets for practices that had become an ingrained part of their normal commuting routine—but were clearly unlawful. Some were stopped for exceeding the posted speed limit, others for failing to signal or for sounding their horns in other than emergency situations. Car pools were drained because of ticketing for overcrowding. Workers got to their jobs late or faced the added expense and problem of traveling on the Long Island Railroad. The highway menace of the law being enforced beyond the pale of established expectations set up a storm of protests— but not to change the law. Within weeks, cops got more time and money to enforce less.

One enterprising commuter who happened to be a lawyer then instituted a class action seeking to enjoin the prosecution of his own and all other cases involving tickets issued during the enforcement campaign. His (perfectly correct) grounds were, essentially, that violators had been passive victims of a police conspiracy. Naturally, the interest of the general public ordained that this suit be dismissed. It was— ostensibly on the grounds that the lawyer had not adequately proven his case. This decision preserved one important function of the judicial process: fostering the image that the law is enforced impartially as written and across the board. Unobeyed, unenforced, and unchanged, the law, because of the police settlement remained an available weapon for social control. And those whose circumstances required them to break it inevitably affirmed their right not to be labeled offenders in the process, by having indirectly pressured the settlement.

This suburban uprising illustrates one way that social norms are fed into the machinery of legal administration: notice was served on the system that a vocal and influential group could not tolerate enforcement, and this message filtered down to those officials who were in charge of negotiating with the police. In terms of law and its enforcement, the essential point is that, in order to get a better contract, patrolmen hit on the tactic of *doing what they were nominally employed to do.* Therefore, they could not be faulted without attention being drawn to the fact that their system —the whole institutional operation of which they were a part—routinely functioned by tolerating illegality. As planned, suddenly enforcing official rules in a literal and even-handed manner spotlighted the law's inadequacy as a mechanism for regulating conditions that actually existed and for coping with the intentions of those who were being governed. It precipitated a confrontation between these rules and the norms of travellers, between the "theory" represented by the law and the practice that the enforcement arm knew and allowed to exist.

Tension had previously been avoided by the expedient of condoning whatever illegal activity the car-driving consumers of police services were believed to have demanded. The traffic laws had, in effect, been amended to conform with the social norms that had emerged in the course of commuting practices. These norms then became legitimated through a pattern of enforcement that, in turn, created in the drivers reciprocal expectations that were not supposed to be unilaterally breached—that is, the enforcement pattern was permitting certain violations to go officially unnoticed and, therefore, unpunished, and the resulting expectation of drivers was that they could commit illegal acts, within limits, and not be considered violators. The screw had one more turn. The reciprocal expectation of police was that it was not their job to run in motorists who broke the law within the recognized, socially accepted limits.

When they began enforcing the law within these limits, they dishonored their part of the bargain for a specific, extra-legal reason: to galvanize a commuter lobby. They made two assumptions about the travellers: first, that even though victimized by strict enforcement, the travellers would still not obey the law; and second, that they would not consider getting it officially changed as one of their alternatives. If these assumptions were correct, then the only course of action the commuters might adopt would be to put pressure on county officials to deal with the cops—in essence, to join with the police in a common front. This, indeed, was done.

The motorists' catalytic effect in causing a bargain to be struck depended on both factions (motorists and police) recognizing that their own jobs and interests were in jeopardy so long as continuation of the dispute meant that certain people were being treated as traffic violators. A stable balance of illegality requires that the law, in practice, exclude from its prohibitions "normally" illegal behavior of particular groups. Fittingly, it was a lawyer who took upon himself the spokesman's job of trying to wring from the courts official acknowledgment of this illegal reality. Nominally, he lost and paid his fines—though at reduced rates that were, inconsistently, then being pegged by "understanding" judges. But while the judiciary was ruling that "a law's a law for all that," something of the opposite was being confirmed in practice. Negotiators were forced to acknowledge that they had reached the limit of administration of the law that did not accommodate to social norms, to what people intended to go on doing anyway. On the roads, if not in the courts, the lawyer's truth was demonstrated—as it had been before the crackdown—that enforcers have only a limited ability to enforce without the at-least-implied consent of certain violators.

We can now take another brief look at the lawyer's unique part in "shady" transactions like the ones illustrated earlier.

The example of the suburban police who went by the book indicated that one way to correct an excessive (non-manageable) disparity between enforced book-law and norms is by the application of pressure on administrators within the system to change the enforcement pattern. The very nature of the lawyer's role makes him another stabilizing force. More than an official of the legal system, he is also blatantly the creature of whatever private interests can afford to hire him. In this go-between capacity, he has a cross-pollinating effect, asserting the standards and norms of the legal system and disseminating awareness of community standards and norms that it must somehow accommodate if it is going to work.

His own knowledge of community norms and standards cannot be just academic. The more he internalizes and personifies them, the more effective a spokesman he is within the law structure. As a representative of some sector of the community, his job is to rationalize its normal operating procedures. In so doing, he cannot avoid adopting, condoning, and, finally, becoming implicated in them. To be sure, in order to survive as a practitioner he has to meet certain formal criteria that are officially accepted as proof that he is keeping his nose clean. But if he really kept his nose clean— as per the requirements for admission to practice—he would be useless to clients, a failure as a lawyer and, therefore, a nullity within the legal structure. Unless he practices in a monastary, all efforts to become successful require the lawyer's developing considerable sophistication in the ways of the world. Dexterity in recognizing and manipulating things as they actually are enables him to manage a client's affairs. "If you're not corrupt, you're a loser."

Finally, in the process of assimilating worldly knowhow with his technical skills, he becomes neutralized as an agent by which the legal structure can change those established norms that are in conflict with the stated law. As a puritan to be let loose on the community, the lawyer is kept reined by his need to maintain the trust of those whose continued patronage is necessary to establish his very credentials as a lawyer. Financial security in his practice does not make him any freer for missionary duties but is a measure of the commitments that he has already made. Financial security is a sign that the lawyer is "safe." His professional limitations as reformer inhere in the fact that he has made it, is on the make, or else is too naïve or insignificant to be listened to seriously.

7

THE PRIVATE TUNES
OF JUSTICE

¶ BAREFOOT BOY WITH CHEEK

At about eight thirty one morning late in June, while I was packing for a week's trip with my family, the telephone rang. A psychiatrist client was calling from his home, in a well-heeled New York City suburb, a tone of urgency in his voice. His eleven-year-old son had just been sent home from the Jewish parochial school he attended. The principal had refused to let him in because the boy wouldn't wear shoes. This day was the semester's last—traditionally, of course, rather light on academics. But, Dad said, that was beside the point: he paid tuition like everyone else; shoes had nothing to do with education; the youngster had every right to be in that school. (Suddenly, I appreciated the generation gap: in my time we had gone about getting autographs on the final day; this youngster started his off principal-baiting and succeeded in getting out early, to boot.)

There could be no doubting the father's rage. "Don't you see," he said. "It's a matter of principle: this strait-laced bastard thinks he can walk all over the kids." Then he came to the point. "Janet and I wanna' sue." "For what?" I asked, surprised. "Money damages—shame, humiliation, mental anguish, embarrassment, and psychic harm. That sort of thing; you know." I asked if he really thought the boy had been emotionally harmed. "Certainly." I could only conjure up the image of the son loafing around home for a few more hours, waiting for his schoolmates to finish up for the year, then, all together, talking over the adventure. "I can get you any psychiatrist to say so, too," he added.

I said a court might issue an order restraining the principal from doing the same thing next year—and agreed to handle the case if he wanted to proceed on that basis—but, I added, this probably wasn't a damages type of suit and, even if it was, I didn't see any injury or loss worth a real award. Still, the medic remained sold on the idea of money damages. "That's the only way this guy will learn his lesson." I tried a different tack—"Bob, there's a good chance you'll get laughed out of court, maybe with a six-cent award"—but he wasn't swayed. "How about the ACLU?" he asked. "Would they take the case?" I said he could try, then reminded him that, if he sued and lost, he might get socked with court costs.

"What you're telling me," he said, exasperatedly, "is that the law is a shoddy farce. Is it Justice to get pushed around and then have to hold your tongue? You're saying the status quo, the establishment, always has the upper hand." It was hard for me to believe what I knew, from his tone-of-voice, was true: that Bob, who had himself come up the hard way, believed he was being perfectly serious.

Somehow, the incipient young radical in the psychiatrist's household had managed, undoubtedly with parental encouragement, to conform to the rules sartorial up to the final moment that formal learning ended in his school. This liberal, free-thinking father was seeking the best of two worlds for his boy: a taste of fashionable protest—a touch of revolution—but, above all, a solid education that would stand him in good stead just in case the old-style credentials were still around in the future. I knew for a fact that this precise combination was very much "in" and encouraged by many well-to-do families. In an earlier generation, their kids got boxing lessons and took hayrides. Though it was unlikely they would end up in the ring or down on the farm, they got a genteel taste of what was going on elsewhere in the world—minus the life-or-death context in which these activities were normally played out.

But the father was unwittingly involved in a "demonstration" of his own: demonstrating the muscle power of the middle class. He had access to a lawyer on-the-spot, at any time, for advice, representation, or even just for show and could make use of this access with the aim of proving to his son or symbolically convincing himself that the old man was sympathetic to social change and social Justice after all. This display of power should have been the boy's most cogent lesson that day. Although I had not been of much help, besides being part of the show—which, considering the boy's stage of oedipal rebellion, may well have been all that Bob was really looking for—there was no doubt that, if he had wanted to start suit immediately, Bob could have gone down a list and summoned and gotten some other lawyer to respond to his wishes. Like his insurance portfolio, his legal coverage was adequate for whatever emergency was likely to arise, even one so frivolous as pursuing money damages for an eleven year old who had missed the last day of private elementary school.

A short time before, 678 black and Puerto Rican students, all at once, were summarily kicked out of a New York City high school—to which they had originally been transferred in order to provide a desired ethnic and racial mix with the school's enrolled white students. The principal who ordered these mass suspensions did so without a warning or hearing and without specific charges of any sort being leveled against them. By the time a court got around to ordering them back, those expelled had lost so much school time that the judge's decision also required the board of education to provide a special compensatory program for them. This was intended to allow a symbolic "make up" (over the summer!) for the education they had missed during the regular school year. Money damages were not sued for in this case.

Ultimately, the principal had gotten what he wanted: "cooling" a situation by causing the energies of his "opponents" to be immediately deflected to the court arena and absorbed in legal processes.

¶ OLD SCHOOL TIES

Up to a short while ago, anyone entering the library of one of New York City's major law schools had to pass a large sign. It was worded, approximately, as follows: ONLY THOSE IN APPROPRIATE PROFESSIONAL ATTIRE

PERMITTED HERE. Of course, a court would strike down any law thus phrased as being unconstitutionally vague. But there was no lack of understanding about its meaning among those who toiled there and little likelihood that it would ever get tested in court. Nor, apparently, did any question exist among librarian-enforcers about how the sign (posted law) should be interpreted. The "appropriate" uniform for male professionals was a coat and tie; for the ladies, skirts or dresses. I never witnessed any protest among library users—lawyers who had already passed muster and students yet to appear before the character committee of the bar association—either about the sign or the librarian's authority to interpret it or enforce some anonymous higher-up's interpretation. The dynamics of this situation bear certain obvious parallels, which will not be belabored, with those at the pier.

Recently, without fanfare, the sign vanished. I telephoned the library to inquire about its passing. A staff member who answered said: "Oh, yes, we simply removed it. Of course, we still expect appropriate attire in the library." He didn't otherwise specify what standards were being applied. From observation, however, it seems clear that the range of acceptable professional attire has broadened.

This trifling episode illustrates something about the process of legal professionalization and, perhaps, about the field itself. It shows how the law changes, *in particulars*, without ever altering its set course and magnetic attraction toward the acceptable and the respectable—whatever, at the moment, these happen to be. As the psychiatrist's case indicates, it became socially "safe" to align oneself on the side of democratization in dress. By the time protest reaches Westchester, the battle is won and only mopping-up operations remain, whose final outcomes cannot be in doubt. The only thing, after all, that was really at stake in both suburbia and the law library was the right of future managers of society to be less than blatant, in the symbolism of their clothing, about their prospects.

Both the future attorney and the lawyer already in practice have to keep a sharp eye out for whatever changes in symbols might affect their employability or business. As quickly as these changes seem established, students, trainers and practitioners alike must adapt to them. It is one of the law school's responsibilities to permit and encourage whatever looks to be necessary for the lawyer-on-the-loose. For an attorney, the image of being ideologically current is as important as the image of success. Law schools, therefore, both in their substantive course-content and in subliminal signals that they radiate about the role of professionals, can be conceived of as institutes for ideological fashions. Designers and instructors alike must, themselves, appear ideologically in vogue. An institute's survival depends on its reputation in such matters, as expressed by the modish phrase "being relevant."

¶ THE ECONOMICS OF CONSCIENCE

As with the law school, large law firms also respond to demands for "change" that, in the long run, rebound to the benefit of the giant commercial interests they serve. So the firms in the coin of the day offer lawyer-workers money, proximity to power, and prestige.

Passing off the money costs to their corporate clients—
and if the clients cannot absorb them, then ultimately, because of the clients' strategic placement in the economy, to
the general public—the major firms encounter no problem
in hiking the salaries of their comparatively small group of
lawyer-employees. But to keep themselves in a position to
continue brain-picking the law schools of recent grads, the
firms are called upon to offer still more. Backed by the relatively limitless resources of their clients, they find this
"more" easy, and actually profitable, to offer—especially
since it can be so readily translated into an investment of
mere money. Currently, prestige and job satisfaction now
include the symbolism of social commitment. No longer are
they solely met by the requirement of an address. Like the
Westchester scion attending school in *deshabille*, the new
lawyers demand another component of status. In response
to this clamor, they now are encouraged, for example, to
work for any political candidate of their choice—by being
given off two weeks a year, with pay.

Such work is their touch of acceptable protest, their hay-
ride, their boxing lesson. Having already indicated their decision to go after power and money through established
channels by becoming associated with the large firms in the
first place, they present little risk as political workers. The
chances are remote that their talents will be devoted to the
service of "unacceptable" candidates, those with goals seriously inimical to the political and economic interests that
these lawyers serve the other fifty weeks of the year.

Traditionally, lawyers hired by the large firms remain at
that level for the rest of their professional lives, float inter-
changeably from one identical firm to another, or else end
up "fired"—by being placed in a lucrative job as house
counsel to their own former clients and continuing, from

their new vantage points, to work closely with the colleagues from their erstwhile firms. Two weeks of politicking is not likely to change this pattern. The payoff to law firms of allowing political participation, then, stays close to home.

This payoff is in the form of employee contentment, and increased "knowhow"—a reservoir of varied professional experiences and personal contacts. All of these enhance a firm's social and political power and, consequently, its potential for asserting client interests. These intangibles will eventually be packaged as legal protection and resold to the very clients who indirectly footed the bill for their original acquisition.

The experience of social "participation"—at least, on levels such as grassroots political campaigning, handling the legal affairs of a corner poverty organization, or offering free representation in the lower criminal courts—is normally most vociferously demanded by a firm's younger lawyers. These are the ones who have not yet become exclusively absorbed in clients' legal matters, immersed in financial dealings or obsessed with their own material self-aggrandizement. They also happen to be the lowest-paid juniors and associates. The considerable amount of potential power and leverage that elite firms acquire when they play along with the idealism of their own Young Turks, therefore, comes cheap.

When powerful law firms respond to the "demands of the times," then, they couldn't care less about social justice or change—except, perhaps, incidentally. What they are actually doing is diversifying the fringe benefits of employment in order to grease their sources of recruitment. They might as well be subscribing to another box at the Met or for the Mets or buying another firm membership in an exclusive athletic club—essentially at no cost to themselves. Their fundamental purpose is to keep themselves in a good position to continue business-as-usual, purveying immunity to powerful corporations.

The irony of this situation is that so many well-intentioned young lawyers, when on their two-weeks "detached duty" as high-paid "volunteers," find themselves once again dealing with the same all-year-round corporate clients—but from a vastly different perspective than as members of their firms.

¶ PERSPECTIVES, PERCEPTIONS AND REFLECTIONS

Children in one fashionable summer camp have their own adaptation of a well-known folk song by Woody Guthrie. Their version goes like this:

> Oh, this is my land,
> It's only my land,
> If you don't get off,
> I'll shoot your head off.
> I got a shot gun,
> And you don't got one:
> This land was made for only me.

Law defends the rights of ownership. We have, literally, sold off most of our corner of the planet and devised a scheme, the law, for the public to defend whatever rape of the land a private owner decides is profitable for him. Almost every public restriction on the use of land can be gotten around. Trees are ripped off and sold. Whatever can be gouged from beneath the surface can be taken. Animals can be killed or sold. People living or working on, or passing through, private land, must pay a tax and toll to its private owners. We accept that the land is theirs. Their families inherit the same rights of consumption, exploitation, eradication, and exclusion. For two hundred years we have countenanced the first grabbers being able to parcel out the country to the highest payers. We have paid our own toll for living on the land and our taxes for a system to enforce the owners' *"rights."*

While for private purposes, the country itself has been dissected, symbols remain to hold us together. We would feel outraged if the Declaration of Independence, say, were auctioned off to a private corporation. Yet we accept a corporation's right of ownership over the actual land simply because it was the highest bidder. It is the symbol that we defend.

Always, if the system is to continue, the weak must believe they are striking some reasonable bargain with the strong. In dealing with symbols and pretense, the law permits this belief. Its social function is to fulfill expectations that in fact cannot be met be in reality, to supply symbols—like the words on an affidavit testifying to an individual's sterling character—that substitute for what really is.

Law thrives on and sustains belief in fantasy. People want to think that some system works enough of the time, for the reason that they then can believe in it. Dr. Bob, for example, closed his eyes to the realities he encountered while slugging his way up from the bottom and, for the first time, found "injustice"—over a pair of shoes, over his son. We accept John's golden smile—and his crime: he's a cop, fighting crime; his victim's a crook. Dr. Bell, lawyers, clients, unions, companies, witnesses, the commuting public sturdily coursing along the arteries of suburbia, all whistle their private tunes of Justice.

II

IN THE MAZE

"It's the Look that Counts"

—Headline from ad in the
New York *Daily News*.

INTRODUCTION

Statutes, lawyers and courts: according to the traditional view, three independent components of the legal system. But the first section of this book indicated how the traditional view of law is largely wishful fiction. Rather than being composed of separable and self-contained elements, the system is actually a network consisting of many real people who are either furiously competing or tenuously co-existing with each other.

We considered both lawyers and the police as representative participants in this network. Mostly viewing themselves through the hazy abstraction of Justice, it nevertheless became clear that, in the final analysis, they actually adapt very practically to existing social norms. In fact, they are usually living examples of these norms. Professionals within the legal system respond pragmatically, not according to any firm concept of Justice but according to their view of what is going to be tolerated and where the pressures will be put. They consider the present distribution of social power, they are "realistic." From this attitude evolves the "law" of political and administrative inertia: *business as usual; treat with the customers as you find them.* All participants in the legal process—cops, clients, lawyers, judges, and others—are guided by these maxims and thus avoid fundamental change by means of the essential technique of adaptation. The law fits into or, at least, does not upset, the expectations of those who give it credibility and lip service. It enforces and is enforced more or less according to who holds the cards. This does not imply that those with whom it must treat are always the same. Power interests sometimes shift, and temporary alliances are often formed. Every group is vigorously in pursuit of power and its own maximum freedom from regulation, and those on top are kept busy defending their status.

In the section to come, our focus changes. No longer are we concerned with what the insiders are doing and how they do it. Instead, we take a look at the *organizational* components of the law—for example, parole agencies, treatment centers, and the courts themselves. Each of these elements generates certain institutional pressures that cause its workers to assume the postures of officialdom, to act as representatives of one or another of law's bureaucracies, and even, sometimes, to serve as personal extensions of these bureaucracies.

We also examine some of the imperatives that cause bureaucracies to scratch each other's backs. Their highly symbiotic relationships are the result of a sort of community of interests, engendering an inevitable conspiracy to maintain a profitable front image for the law. This symbiosis is also caused, as we shall see, by the very differences in, or conflicts between, the methods, goals, and needs for survival of each of the bureaucracies.

Society invents many ways to intervene in and exert control over the lives of individuals. Organizations are then established to implement these interventions. Usually, the organizations function under a banner of ideals—for example, rehabilitating criminals or resolving personal or commercial disputes through "rational" means instead of by force. The workers in these organizations normally become infused with the particular beliefs that are appropriate for their group's ideals.

But as soon as an organization is set up, its professed goals are automatically pressed into the service of the practical goal of organizational self-perpetuation. The group becomes primarily concerned with securing a place for itself within an existing hegemony of bureaucracies. It does this, in short, by finding and maintaining a supply of customers for whatever service it offers.

In the legal system, the source for customers usually turns out to be other organizations loosely confederated within the same system. They each are constituted on a processing-out technique whereby one organization's recruits, obtained from somewhere else, are passed on to the next organization. An organization's success then gets measured in terms of how many customers it can take in and later pass on. When a law bureaucracy seems to have solved its "sales problem," found a reason for being, all it is really concerned with is its rate of human ingestion and expulsion—which it uses as justification for continuing its activities and expanding them.

Our concern in this second section will be with the individual who gets caught up in these bureaucracies. His treatment is determined according to how he affects, or can be used to serve, organizational needs and interests. What counts in deciding his fate, so far as he can control it, is whether or not he is capable of picking up on what rules are just for show and which ones really matter—for the organization's sake—and his willingness, or ability, to play by these rules. If he is going to have a relatively painless experience while being processed through a bureaucracy, he must seem to accept a role that is convenient for the organization. This is true whether his participation is voluntary—say, as a civil litigant—or coerced—perhaps as a prisoner. And he must understand and accept the fact that ideological goals are window-dressing.

8

THE CORRECTORS

¶ **ON PAROLE**

ON MY HONOR
I WILL DO MY BEST
TO DO MY DUTY TO GOD
AND MY COUNTRY
AND TO OBEY THE SCOUT LAW
TO HELP OTHER PEOPLE
AT ALL TIMES,
TO KEEP MYSELF PHYSICALLY
STRONG, MENTALLY AWAKE
AND MORALLY STRAIGHT.
—Boy Scout *Oath*

When paroled into the custody of the (recently defunct) New York City Parole Commission, all adolescent reformatory and adult penitentiary prisoners signed the "Rules and Conditions of Parole." These are typical of terms for parole used in every jurisdiction throughout the country. Considered in context, they cannot be observed literally or according to their "spirit." Although reasonable enough on the surface, their actual use has little to do with their apparent intent. Like most laws, they are implemented so as to further the organization that is charged with administering them.

a. I will make a reasonable attempt to earn my own living, to respect the rights of others, to support my dependents, if any, and satisfy any just claims upon my time and income.

b. I will make no effort to conceal my activities, whether by failure to report them or by falsely reporting them or by hampering any investigation of them by the Parole Commission, and I will not marry without first obtaining the permission of my parole officer.

c. I will report to my parole officer at the time and place specified on my report card. If I fail to report in person as directed, I will, without delay, write to my parole officer . . . explaining why I failed to appear and will then report the next day. . . .

d. I will not use or engage in the sale of narcotics in any form and must abstain from any over-indulgence in intoxicating liquors.

e. At all times, I will keep my parole officer informed of the address at which I live and any other information which will help him finding me at any time. I will notify him before removing to a new address, and I will reply promptly to any communication from my parole officer or other officials of the Parole Commission.

f. I will not leave the city without first obtaining the consent of my parole officer. Should I wish to accept employment out of town, I will produce written proof that I have been offered a job before I may expect to get the officer's consent to leave.

g. At all times, I will fully explain how I meet my expenses. If my income includes gifts from friends, odd jobs, repayment of debts or similar irregular income, I will keep a record of it, including the names and addresses of the persons concerned, and be ready to report it to my parole officer.

h. I agree to continue to receive medical treatment for any social disease and to attend a mental hygiene clinic if so directed by my parole officer. If I should contract any communicable disease, I will report this to the parole officer, will secure medical treatment, and will make every effort to prevent the spread of the infection.

i. I will keep reasonable hours, but this does not prevent me from working nights or from engaging in any approved occupation. I am not required to tell anybody I am on parole, but I must avoid going anywhere late at night without a good reason.

j. I will avoid undesirable friends or acquaintances and especially anyone having a criminal record. I am aware that my visiting or writing to anyone in prison, no matter what the excuse, will be considered a violation of my parole.

k. I will show to my parole officer my Social Security card, food handler's certificate, union card, public relief card, etc., if I secure any. Under no circumstances will I apply for a hunting license or a chauffeur's or operator's license without first obtaining permission of my parole officer. If I receive such consent and secure a license, I will show it to my parole officer.

l. If I am arrested in another state during my parole period, I hereby agree to waive extradition and not resist being returned by the Parole Commission to the City of New York.

These terms are blatantly incompatible with the requirements for survival that most parolees face. Most obviously, some conditions must be broken if others are kept. For example, when meeting his officer or entering a parole counseling group, the parolee has to consort with persons in the category of "undesirable friend or acquaintance and especially anyone having a criminal record." More importantly, aside from such conditions that are impossible in their own terms, most of the others cannot be enforced even when their violation is practically waved under the officer's nose. This is the basic problem. For example, skipping appointments is an infraction that justifies returning the parolee to jail. It is also a strong indication that he is up to other forbidden actions and doesn't want to confess them to his officer—two separate violations in their own right. If he comes in and lies, conceals, or doesn't voluntarily disgorge his sins—and then gets found out—he is supposed to land back in jail. If he follows the rules and tells the truth, he places the officer in an uncomfortable position that can only cause more trouble: the officer who knows has to do something or else he, too, becomes implicated. Either he turns over his charge to the police for a new prosecution or returns him to prison as a parole violator.

The listing of the "Rules and Conditions" is preceded by this statement:

> I,_____, No._____, having been paroled this day, promise that I will comply with all the conditions of parole described below and *any other conditions* imposed by the Parole Commission [italics mine]. I realize that a violation of any of these conditions may result in my return to the institution for the balance of my commitment.

And it ends with this acknowledgment:

> I have carefully read the above instructions, agree to them fully *and have received oral instructions from the parole officer explaining them and what is expected of me while on parole* [italics mine].
>
> Date: _____ Signed:_____
>
> In Presence of _____
>
> Parole Officer

In most jurisdictions, parole bureaucracies are crammed with lawyers and legal advice. For example, all three New York City parole commissioners had practiced law and some officers were former law students. The New York organization also had at its disposal the services of the city's separate law department.

Despite the availability of this legal talent, the commission's "Rules and Conditions" document was meaningless when considered by normal contractual standards. It failed to conform even to minimal requirements of public policy— for example, that a party to an agreement not be subject to duress, that minors cannot enter into agreements with the city by themselves, and that no one can bind himself to comply with something so vague as "any other conditions" that might be promulgated in the future. It exacted an advance waiver of the privilege against self-incrimination, of the rights to free speech, assembly, and due process, and to normal liberties such as traveling interstate, marrying, entering civil contracts, selecting employment or not working at all, and receiving or declining medical, psychological, and psychiatric (including shock and drugs) treatment. By and large, except for the fact of imprisonment, the parolee appeared in worse legal shape than he was in as an inmate.

Aside from the document's probable lack of legal validity,

both sides knew that its prescriptions and conditions would and could not be followed. Part of the hidden relationship that it set in motion actually depended on this fact.

In theory, a parolee, like an inmate, has only watered-down constitutional rights. And in practice there are few restrictions on any officer's authority to return his man to prison during the parole period. Therefore, there was, in effect, no practical reason why the "Rules and Conditions" *should* be legally binding and valid. In fact, at first glance, there was no reason for them at all, much less for the formality of dating, the exercise of signing, the ritual of witnessing, or for ponderous legal phraseology and repetitive detail.

But this paper did more than reinforce the parolee's awareness of his officer's legal power. Its main effect—and that of similar documents abounding in parole groups everywhere—was to facilitate the administration of a going operation, the parole organization. Of the twelve rules and conditions imposed in New York, for example, eight of them—those requiring full disclosure of all the parolee's activities, income, associations, employment, and residence, and eliciting his promise to report to the officer regularly—specifically and exclusively eased and expedited the officer's basic job of conducting his apparent surveillance. Their upshot was to hinder the parolee's forming any relationship with another person or agency that might cut into the officer's need for information or blunt his Sword of Damocles, the threat of jail. In other words, the main thrust of parole conditions is to force cooperation with the officer in perpetuating the existing parole system, and has little to do with behavior.

A parole officer actually has few options. Prisons are in crisis and manage to function only because nobody can really stomach a good look at what goes on within them. Mass returns to jail would surely herald their total collapse. In fact, a hidden, but major, consideration in deciding any inmate's "eligibility" for parole is always the prison's need to make room for new arrivals. Just as a certain number must be declared eligible—with code phrases like "a good candidate for rehabilitation and adjustment to the community"—parole officers and commissioners are fully aware of a practical limit on how many parolees they can reinstitutionalize without tipping the boat. If they exceed this limit they will call attention to themselves—ostensibly as faulty rehabilitators—and cast public doubt on the parole system's inherent ability to cut down on "recidivism." Professionally speaking, behind phrases about recidivism lie the prison system's unspoken complaint that its sister service, parole, with whom it is fiercely competitive for a share of the public budget, is not juggling its own share of the caseload—with which neither really knows what to do.

On the other hand, parolees cannot be allowed to remain at large while totally ignoring the rules of parole. An officer's main job is to compile and record information. The enormous size of his caseload prevents him from doing much of this in person. He must depend, instead, on a technique that produces confessions. His spot checks in "the field" reinforce his status by creating the impression that he can verify anything the parolee tells him. But, like the Wizard of Oz, the officer's success ultimately depends upon his being able to maintain a minimum of parolee-faith in his, the officer's, omnipotence and on his ability to fool the parolee. His charge must be impressed with the officer's apparently unlimited re-jailing powers and, to a lesser extent, believe that the officer has world enough and time to verify what is actually happening in the parolee's private business and life. For this system to work, the officer has to hear mostly plausible stories, and the parolee has to maintain some façade of compliance.

A parole officer is constantly involved in assessing the possibility that a parolee under his supervision will break contact with him and lose himself in the community. If one does and is later picked up on sensational new charges, the officer has exposed his commissioners—with consequences that are likely to come home to roost. His main concern, then, is keeping in some kind of touch with his caseload and protecting himself with entries in the file.

From the parolee's point of view, a relationship with an officer is unnatural and, essentially, undesirable. How, then, does he get co-opted into fulfilling the needs of the system and playing an indispensable part in it?

What goes on is similar to the dynamics of "settling" a negligence case and is in the same genre as the method by which prosecutors get defendants to cop pleas. At stake is the survival of the parole system and the officer's own job. On the other side, the parolee is playing for his continued liberty.

The first ingredient in the mix is precisely a set of rules that will, inevitably, be violated by the parolee. Those "Rules and Conditions" not directly dealing with the parole system's own smooth operation serve the function of establishing impossible demands. They set a standard of virtue that the Disciples themselves would have trouble meeting and that average parolees, with the usual resources of ex-convicts, are sure to find hopelessly unrealistic.

At the same time, the individual officer has to be given the power to apply, interpret, and enforce these conditions. This is made clear when the parolee acknowledges, in writ-

ing, that he has "received oral instructions from the . . .
officer explaining [the rules] and what is expected of me
while on parole"—notwithstanding that what is ostensibly
expected has been spelled out in twelve paragraphs immediately preceding.

The conditions of parole, then, cannot be objectively determined if the system of parole is going to work. The officer
must be able to make judgments about what constitutes "re-
specting the rights of others," what amounts to alcoholic
"over-indulgence," what is "good reason" for being late,
and which friends are "undesirable."

The bargain that is struck permits a successful parolee to
lead the kind of life that he knows how to live in spite of
rules that seem to require his conforming to virtues that are
irrelevant and to standards that are unrealistic. In exchange,
he gives the system what it really wants, periodic contacts
that enable the officer to maintain records and avoid having
to play the impossible role of a St. Bernard in the ghetto.

A few years ago I headed a federally sponsored rehabilitation project that involved intensive dealings with New York
City's parole organization. Just before the research got un-
funded, we held a conference of parole officers who had
worked on the project. A few remarks that were made at
that time illuminate the phenomenon that we are discussing—bureaucratic self-preservation in law:

SENIOR SUPERVISING PAROLE OFFICER: We think a
man has failed on parole when he either becomes a technical violator or an arrest violator. More so, I would say, a
technical violator because here he is on the street, he disappears, he stops reporting, he breaks off relationship with his
parole officer. When he gets arrested, maybe for many reasons—it may be a circumstantial situation where later on he

is reinstated for parole—but when he just absconds and re-
fuses to cooperate, then, of course, I think his failure there is
a little bit more significant than a man who is arrested. . . .

These rules and regulations [for parole] that are set forth
are not hard and fast. They are flexible. As long as the officer
maintains some type of contact with the subject who is on
parole, we will not come up and declare him delinquent unless there are some overt acts of delinquent behavior. . . .

So you see, there is no definite line here [about what kind
of illegal activities we tolerate from parolees]. We are depending on the boy [the young parolee]. We will go to all
lengths [not to send him back to jail] so long as he makes his
reports and comes in. . . . Now, here is the point: if, when,
he disappears completely and breaks off with parole, now at
that point, then, he really becomes an absconder [parole vio-
lator] and we have to take some action.

PROJECT DIRECTOR: Well, suppose he periodically reports to you but doesn't come in [meet his appointments
with his officer] when he should *all* the time?

SENIOR SUPERVISING PAROLE OFFICER: No. We
can't permit that. He must come in. He may not come in as
regularly as he should, but he has got to come in.

The "Rules and Conditions" of parole should properly be
seen as a sort of tip sheet. The savvy parolee uses them for a
guide to the limits of safe conversation with his officer. They
indicate what answers may and should be put "on the record" if he wants to stay out of jail and avoid provoking the
officer into excessive poking around, both in conference and
in "the field." By a ratio of eight to four—in New York City,
at least—the rules also underscore that what counts is not so
much what the parolee does as how conscientiously he reports to his officer and what he says when he gets there.

Handing the parolee a written set of outlandish conditions at the start gives the officer leverage. He can say that "these are the rules"—already printed, none of his doing—appear sympathetic and agree to stretch them a bit—for an implied price of cooperation. The ritual of the parolee's signing the document then puts the officer firmly in the driver's seat. When the parolee makes a written "promise" that he knows he can't keep—and on which his freedom seems to depend—he has left for himself only the hope of making it with his officer. That the name of the game is not making the officer's job too difficult is actually spelled out for him. The parolee is told, in writing, to "realize that a violation of *any* of these conditions *may* result in . . . return to the institution" [italics added]. In other words, everything depends on the officer. The parolee gets what is really important in "oral instructions" explaining "what is expected." If discreet, he can do what he wants ("there is no definite line here"), with the officer going "to all lengths" not to stand in his way—"so long as he makes his reports and comes in."

Given the helplessness of parole to effect any fundamental changes, this bargain makes tactical sense. The situation that existed in New York is representative. About a year before it was integrated into the state system, the city organization was supervising a total of 4,777 parolees. To handle these, it had three commissioners (one of whom, it so happened, was incapacitated over four months of the twelve), officers with a caseload of around one hundred each, and a wide territory to be covered. A system with "flexibility"—where parolees do most of the work—is an absolute necessity under these typical conditions.

But not every parolee is resourceful enough to read the numerous signals to the effect that he need only play the game. Some become overwhelmed at their deviation from the fantasy norms of parole and frightened about continuing to meet their officers. Others equate freedom of action with the liberty not to report. These individuals soon pay a high price for their inability to adapt to the system's demands. Because their behavior embarrasses the organization by confronting officers with the inherent impossibility of doing their job, they get put out of sight—like any unpleasant reminder—back in jail. But those who are sharp enough to recognize and gratify the bureaucracy's interest in perpetuating itself get chalked up as being properly supervised and, finally, enter the lists of the "rehabilitated." Although this label does not correspond to any consequence of the parole experience, it permits parolees to perform a final service to the system by becoming statistical ammunition for the organizations' next budget request.

¶ IN "THE CONCEPT"

It was my first day back from vacation.

"This nineteen-year-old Negro got caught selling heroin to his friends and we've got the case, they caught him dead-to-rights on three counts but I think the DA would be willing to take a plea on a misdemeanor—or else we can get 'youthful offender' treatment—because the kid's clean, no record!"

The speaker was a young lawyer whom we were "employing," without pay, for the summer. He was teaching

in elementary school in order to beat the draft and wanted
"law experience" for the time when his two years would be
up. Almost unsupervised thus far in his first case, he was obviously proud of how things were going. After adjourning
the pleading until my return, he had browsed at the district
attorney's to see what he "could get" and now, clearly, envi-
sioned no more salutary or suitable ending than for the defendant to seize upon this opportunity that he had been able
to wrest from the government. He had two clincher points:
"You've already made arrangements for the whole fee, anyway, and the kid will probably be able to get a suspended
sentence."

These were very telling reasons. To them I added that it
was August and the court not air-conditioned.

Yet the DA seldom put all his cards on the table this early
in the game, and he was probably even less likely to have
done so when dealing with a greenhorn lawyer. Politically,
too, something might be going for us. During New York's
outdoor summer drug festival, the police are always busy
busting kids in the parks. This is as easy as fishing in a
stocked pond. But it had probably occurred to somebody in
City Hall that to allow half the minors in New York to acquire criminal records would be calamitous or, at least, inconsistent with the many precautions that were then being
taken by the city administration in the hope of missing out
on the season's riots. I therefore suspected that, by waiting,
we could somehow do a little better than pleading guilty to
a misdemeanor. Besides, as a considered assessment of legal
probabilities, the phrase "dead-to-rights" hadn't rung true.
It sounded more like verbal spadework, a rehearsal of advocacy to persuade the client to accept a deal that the lawyer
had already worked out for him. Finally, since our temporary associate had graduated directly from law to grammar

school, I also wondered how much the settlement being proposed might reflect his feeling that it was wrong for pushers, even clients, to get off altogether.

However, I soon concurred that Barry had, after all, been caught "dead-to-rights." The next step was to speak to the assistant prosecutor in charge of drug cases that involved "young" people too old for the juvenile courts. He listened courteously to what was, overall, a familiar pitch: the "youngster" had no criminal record, lived with his intact family in the ghetto, had a brother in the military (who cared enough to come up with cash bail), wasn't yet a full-fledged addict, might someday finish the last year of high school, had been fairly steadily employed, wasn't directly in the rackets but had been dealing just to keep himself supplied with drugs. And, most important, he wanted a chance to rehabilitate himself. Having cleared in advance that Barry preferred "treatment" to jail, I told the assistant DA that my client now wanted to enter a narcotics "rehab" program.

He shook his head. "That'll be hard. There aren't many places that he can get in if he's not an actual addict. No one knows what to do with these offenses, really."

I was struck by the overlap that the law system provided. Here was a prosecutor somewhat concerned about social problems and back in my office was the client's first defense lawyer with a subconscious investment in punishment.

An arrangement was made for the case to be transferred to a "confidential" part (or courtroom) presided over by a "special" judge. When the court date arrived, Barry and I presented ourselves in a tiny room that had obviously been jerry-built from a robing chamber. Cases were called in one at a time. A young woman assistant DA was "working the part," her role being to safeguard the prosecutor's office

from criticism, get the court itself off the hook, avoid convictions, and motivate defendants to stay out of trouble—
preferably out of the city—for some respectable time.

"Your honor," she began. "This is a very serious felony
charge—selling heroin. But the defendant has requested
one chance to get himself rehabilitated and, after investigat-
ing all the circumstances of the case, the People are inclined
to go along. We will consent to a two-week adjournment. If,
by then, the defendent can get himself into a rehabilitation
center, we would consent to further adjourning the case so
long as he stays in treatment successfully. However, I have
made it clear to the defendant's attorney that if the defendant is not successful and doesn't cooperate with the program, or if he should leave before finishing, a warrant for his
arrest will be issued, the case will be re-called immediately
and prosecution pressed. On these conditions we do not op-
pose an adjournment at this time. His mother and father are
in court, your honor, and they also understand these terms."

"Very well," the judge nodded. Looking down at the defendant, he asked, "Young man, do you understand that
you've got to get admitted to some rehabilitation program
before this case comes up again?" Barry: "Yes, sir." "And do
you also understand that we're going to continue with the
trial if you flunk out of it?" "Yes, sir." The judge then
turned to the squat, inscrutable black woman standing on
one side of her son. "Are you the mother?" "Yes, judge."
"Do you understand what is happening?" "Yes, judge." "Do
you consent?" "Yes, judge." "Very well," he contined. "The
court adjourns this case two weeks on defendant's request."

The assistant DA joined us in the hallway outside the
courtroom. She gave me the names of two residential treatment programs, one in a rural upstate community and the
other in Connecticut. Then she turned to Barry. "If you

finish, we're going to recommend dropping this case. But if not, we're going to trial. They send your lawyer regular reports about how you're doing, and I will be notified the minute you leave. Good luck."

She re-entered the courtroom. I could see another defendant before the bench and, as the door shut slowly, heard her begin again: "Your honor . . ."

Barry was eventually accepted into the Connecticut outpost of one of the nation's best-known residential treatment programs, whose main headquarters were in New York City. Almost immediately upon his arrival I began getting monthly progress reports (reproduced here without grammatical editing). This was the first:

November 1, 1968

. . . We are a rehabilitation center for ex-narcotic addicts and our program usually takes from 18 months to 2 years for recovery.

Barry has already begun the long process of learning about his behavior and how to be a responsible, involved individual. . . .

Sincerely yours,
Co-Director

Toward the end of the month, it happened that this same organization became a news item worthy of the front page of the *New York Times*. The several news articles that appeared over the next few weeks related the following, fast-breaking story.

A majority of the group's directors charged the executive with trying to turn the treatment program into a "New Left commune." The board chairman announced that he was requesting sponsoring government agencies to withhold funds from the program until the dispute could be settled. To prevent all money sources from drying up, the field of battle was extended to a Greenwich Village theater that was staging a play about addiction—with ex-addict actors—and donating the profits to the center. Two rival casts lined up, respectively, behind the executive and the board; each laid claim to the stage and, they hoped, to the profits that the performances were generating.

A certain Dr. X, well-known ally of the board chairman, announced that both sides were overemphasizing "ideological" issues and that the crux of the matter was really that the executive had been loading his relatives and friends onto the payroll and was, moreover, generally refusing to carry out the board's directives.

The executive and his staff of sixty-one loyalists resigned en masse, then comandeered the organization's four living facilities and five storefronts. The board publicly announced that it was considering legal action to recover the premises, while the insurgents stated that they too were planning on going into court—to legalize the takeover.

Dr. X., meantime, accepted a board appointment as interim executive—having as yet, however, no territory over which to rule.

The board then formally accepted the old executive's resignation as part of a formula to resolve the entire dispute. Decisions on the resignations of the sixty-one staff members were reserved, as part of the same plan, while three prominent citizens were called in to resolve other outstanding issues. The erstwhile executive was then asked by the board to disassociate himself altogether from the program by physically removing himself from one of the centers, which he was occupying.

Instead of complying, he and the sixty-one staff members

began a sit-in, announcing they had not resigned from the treatment "communities" but merely from the board's control, whose president they accused of underhanded tactics.

Dr. X, switching sides, then proclaimed that he had been "sold out" by the board. Allegedly it had reneged on a pledge to give him full control over the program. His joining the rebellious staff members was scored by the board.

During this time, there was a slight gap in the center's reports about Barry. Then they started again:

January 31, 1969

. . . Due to the fact that we have been trying to establish ourselves in Connecticut, the progress reports have fallen behind. We have restructured our New Haven facility, and the monthly reports will resume again.

At the present time Barry is working on our maintenance department but he has come a step up and is now assuming the position of Ram-Rod. This job entails various responsibilities and enables him to deal with people. Barry has a good attitude. He is now in the position to teach his newer brothers and sisters what he has learned, thereby, reinforcing himself.

If Barry should decide to leave, you will be notified by phone.

Sincerely yours,
Resident Director

February 27, 1969

. . . At this time he is ramrod of the service crew. This job is an important one, particularly because it entails being responsible for the newer brothers. It involves being a leader and giving direction. Barry has become much more open to people and is learning about himself and others.

March 31, 1969

. . . At this time Barry is working in our Expediting Office. The job entails being aware of people in the enviornment, the attitude, learning how to give directions, and assuming a posture as an older member of [the program]. Barry seems to be handling the responsibility very well.

If Barry should decide to leave, you will be notified by mail and phone.

Sincerely yours,
Resident Director

April 30, 1969

. . . Barry is presently working in our department called the expeditors office as an expeditor trainee. This is a position that entails great responsibility. Barry is showing that he can deal with the responsibility given him. Barry is now learning about himself along with others.

Sincerely yours,
Resident Director

From the May report I again learned about the expeditor's office:

May 30, 1969

. . . Barry is presently working in our department called the expeditors office as an expeditor. This is a position that entails great responsibility. Barry is showing that he can deal with the responsibility given him. Barry is now learning about himself along with others.

Sincerely yours,
Resident Director

There was no letter in June. Then came July:

July 23, 1969

. . . Presently Barry is working through a slight set back. There is nothing to be alarmed at as this is an enviornment where we learn to grow up and these situations are expected. Barry does recognize his mistake and will utilize this to his benefit in the future. He has a good attitude.

Depending upon his consistency, will he progress to the point he should be. If Barry should decide to leave before his completion of our program, you will be notified by phone and mail.

Sincerely yours,
Resident Director

I later learned that the "set back" was Barry's unauthorized two-hour sojourn in the nearest town. The program requires residents to remain on the premises during their entire stay in treatment, obviously to allay the fears and minimize the resistance of the native populace.

October 27, 1969

. . . Recently, Barry has moved up another step and has earned the position of Secretary of Operations. This job entails various responsibilities. Barry had made some substantial changes since his re-entry date. He is in a teaching capacity and may utilize his growth by teaching other residents. Barry is well on his way to becoming a well rounded mature man. He has a good attitude and does recognize changes he has yet to make for himself, and he has started to make an effort to change them.

If Barry should decide to leave before his completion of our program, you will be notified by phone or mail.

Sincerely yours,
Resident Director

I inquired about a possible release for Barry.

November 5, 1969

This letter is in reference to your letter of October 21, 1969, in which you requested the release date of Barry.

Barry has been in the Concept for a little over a year. During this time he has made a lot of changes for himself, in our evaluation Barry is well on his way to becoming a well rounded responsible adult. But in order for his growth to continue he will have to be involved for at least another year. I don't know if you were informed when Barry first entered the program that it is a 18 to 24 month program depending on the individual.

We feel that the completion of our program will be the most beneficial to his future.

Sincerely yours,
Assistant Director

November 17, 1969

This letter is to inform you of Barry's situation.

I received your November 10, 1969 letter stating Barry's present legal situation [that his case was coming up once again]. Taking into consideration the information you forwarded [suggesting that the director recommend that the charges finally be dismissed even though treatment was still continuing] I feel you may come to a better understanding if I explain what has motivated him to continue our program.

Just a few weeks ago he was going to leave our program without the consent of the staff, the only reason he decided against this was due to the fact that we informed him his charges were not dismissed, contrary to what he [erroneously] thought.

Due to this, we recommend that he be on probation until

the termination of our program. If he should decide to leave before his completion of our program, you will be notified by phone or mail.

Sincerely yours,
Regional Director

December 3, 1969

. . . This letter is to inform you that Barry left . . . on December 2, 1969 without the consent of the staff.

During the time he was a resident he seemed involved in what [the program] does, although he did not believe in it's effectiveness. He did not have the trust he needed to open up and confront the fears which had led him into his previous negative direction. Barry was resistent to change and did not make an honest effort to become totally involved. Due to this and his lack of trust, he chose to act off his fears and leave.

Sincerely yours,
Resident Director

Barry appeared, unannounced, at my office about an hour before I got this last letter.

"It got so I couldn't take it no more," he said vaguely. "What goes on there you wouldn't believe. Maybe it's right for addicts, but not me. I figured I'm off drugs and not going back, so what's the use of playing?" Supposedly he had lined up a meat-cutting apprenticeship and his father would get him into Harlem Prep (a school that prepared dropouts for college) in September.

When he left, I wrote the prosecutor that Barry looked pretty good and suggested that she might want to see him. There was no reply.

The case came up in court, in its regular turn, three months later. By now, the woman assistant DA had gotten married and entered private practice. Her successor, a male just as solicitous, adjourned the case for another three months, explaining to me that he was "a little worried" about what a judge would make of that last letter from the center. "Get me some proof about Barry's job and Harlem Prep. And make sure he stays clean until June. We'll dismiss then, when it's airtight." And he did.

¶ THE POLITICS OF CORRECTION— AND ONE FUNCTION OF LAW

Parole and treatment are two approaches to "correction" —both coercive. Both are infused with the idea that law can control behavior without having to be too physically brutal. The assumption is that the threat alone is sufficient. Parole arose from nothing more than a desire to keep tabs on those who got executive clemency and were pardoned before their terms expired. Rehabilitation, an older notion, stems from when charitable associations began sending their representatives into prisons to "reform" convicts—and to size them up for free labor. The idea gathered official steam in the United States around the turn of the century with the introduction into this country of separate courts and holding centers for juveniles. It was later picked up by prison employees, who got tired of being patsies—janitors taking care of the garbage—and wanted a better image for themselves than as mere guards and turnkeys. At about the same time a batch of new "helping" professions, that laid claim to being able to reshape minds and lives—especially of those in captivity—seized on the watchword rehabilitation and thereby developed a rationale for their own missionary doings.

No two professionals agree, except superficially, about exactly what constitutes correction. And there is no way to determine validly any effects of rehabilitation or, for that matter, whether or not there are any effects. Explaining the purposes and dynamics of correction, then, is a favorite pastime for purveyors of all sorts of political, psychological, and sociological doctrine.

Because no one ever gets conclusively proven wrong, the notion of correcting people is useful for justifying a whole range of steps taken by the "ins" of society against dissenters of all hues and shades. These steps normally function either to set the dissenters straight or to put them out of the way. Many diverse corrective and rehabilitational efforts have in common only their apparent effect of homogenizing or cowing certain segments of the population and of tranquilizing others. For those on society's outer fringes, getting corrected can result in becoming silenced. Or the intransigents will be labeled dangerous because unreformed. Upon release, their potential "negative" influence is either neutralized by officially imparted stigma or eradicated through satisfactory reformation. In these and other ways, the outcasts of society must elect either to be co-opted in or starved out—in either case being rendered relatively inoperative as dissenters or disrupters.

In order to dispel any possible impression of either chauvinism or xenophobia, I note in passing that the link-up between penal law and mental science knows no national boundaries. A *Times of London* dispatch recently appearing in the *New York Times* is typical of reports that the interested browser may frequently encounter:

On Feb. 5, 1969, Natalya Gorbanevskaya—the Soviet poet who recently was committed to a mental hospital for a second time and declared insane after being accused of anti-Soviet slander—sent a letter signed by 170 people to the Soviet leaders, the Supreme Court and the Prosecutor General. It protested against the trials of dissident intellectuals.

Two days later she fell ill and was admitted to a maternity hospital with the diagnosis: "Pregnancy of 25–26 weeks, anemia, danger of miscarriage." After about a week she was transferred to a mental hospital and even after she was discharged she remained uncertain whether the K.G.B., or secret police, had been responsible.

She later described her fears and experiences in a number of harrowing letters that have been published in the Russian emigre journal *Possev*.

In the excerpts reprinted in the *Times*, Miss Gorbanevskaya recounts how she wanted to sign out of the maternity hospital but came to discover that she was being transferred, instead, to a mental institution. Later she learned:

The next day, Feb. 16, two of my friends came to the maternity hospital convinced that they were going to take me home. My name was not among those who were being discharged. In the maternity hospital they were told that there was no one of that name.

Eventually they managed to talk to the deputy to the chief doctor, who told them that I had been taken to the Kaschenko Psychiatric Hospital.

"Why?" "Well, you see, she was behaving rather strangely."

With great difficulty, they managed to discover what was meant by my "rather strange" behavior. "She kept asking to be discharged and refused to eat."

On Feb. 17 the consultant doctor [at the mental institution] told my mother that I did not need any treatment and that they would discharge me not later than Thursday.

They studied my case history from 1959, talked to me and asked in astonishment "Why did they send you to us?"

"I should like to know that myself," I said.

Chinese labor camps, employing group therapy techniques that we call brainwashing, were once far and away the world's most advanced, best organized, and seemingly successful centers for promulgating mental health through corrective rehabilitation. However, the use of tranquilizers, for "aggressives" and selected others in American prisons (as well as the permissive use of drugs in American ghettos), has now put us in the vanguard. China was able to steal this early march on the occident because its ideological and actual, immediate goals coincided. Its labor camps and psycho-manipulative therapy were concededly run for political purposes. But American rehabilitators cannot yet own up, even to themselves, to goals such as political conformity, permanent menial labor for the poor, publicly supported protection of private commercial interests, and adulation of political leaders. This would be taboo because contrary to our ideology of individualism, class mobility, equal protection by and access to the law—and, most importantly, the right of dissent.

The function of correctional procedures can be understood in light of the goals of the legal system. Every organization develops measures for its own evaluation. Normally, its immediate, actual goals are used to justify its activities. To take the most obvious example: a company whose immediate goal is to make money uses total sales and per-unit profits as its criteria of success. But for such an evaluation, one needs a concrete, measurable goal. When the goal is ideological—for example, doing something that is "right," "good," or "American"—it cannot provide a yardstick to determine the efficiency of a system. An ideological goal is incapable of proving or disproving an organization's success or indicating how, why, and when the organization should change. This is not to say that such a goal has no usefulness. Its function: to provide rationalizations for whatever activity is being undertaken.

Most organizations have both specific and ideological goals. What links the two together is faith. For example, a company may have a specific goal of making money and an ideological one of supporting the American Way of Life. No relationship between these two can be established unless observable behavior or measurable effects are *arbitrarily* equated with and taken as an indication of the ideological goal, the American Way of Life. For example, as proof that making money enhances the American Way of Life, it could be cited that many children from families employed by a company that is making money go to college. But there can only be a consensus of faith rather than any evidence to connect an activity, like going to college, with the ideological goal whose existence it is supposed to prove. The only way an ideological goal can be established by a specific one is for people to *believe* that a connection exists.

Fairness and Justice are the ideological goals of law. Every bureaucracy that is a component of the legal system —such as parole and probation organizations, treatment centers, police departments, courts, and prisons—is committed to some ideological correlate of these goals: reform, rehabilitation, correction, punishment, stopping crime. The correlates are also abstractions that are incapable of telling managers how bureaucracies should be run, much less what their purpose should be. But they do offer a vocabulary in which both those within and outside the system can express their faith that whatever is being done or contemplated is justifiable or else that it should be opposed. This function of an ideology is made possible by the fact that there is no way to prove or disprove any causal connection between it and a particular activity.

Ideological goals are equally useable by advocates of change and by those who favor standing pat. The same ideological goal can easily serve as rhetoric for advocates of opposing alternatives. A system with only ideological goals can conduct any activity so long as those in control sustain their belief that the system is functioning to advance these goals.

The salient characteristic of our legal system is that, contrary to appearances, its stated goals are purely ideological. Law bureaucracies have no acknowledgable, specific, immediate goals that can be related to their activities and processes. This absence of specific goals can be demonstrated by pressing for answers to two questions about the activities of any of the law's bureaucracies: "Why are you doing what you are doing—what is the imperative?" and "How do you know that this activity will achieve the aim you say you have?" There is in law no counterpart to the relationship between activities and goals that exists in business, say, between the specific goal of making money and the specific activity of selling a product. No concrete purposes but only ideological ones predetermine what happens to the prisoner, defendant, parolee, or addict being moved through whatever stages of the law operation that happen to be set up for him. The gap between activities and aims is bridged by faith in legal ideology rather than by the logic of a specific, testable goal.

What is actually done within the legal system is anything

for which the belief can be mustered. A particular activity must be tolerated as somehow furthering the aims of the law—accepted without empirical standards but according to a standard of faith. Ironically, it is law's total commitment to ideology and its lack of specific goals that permit the system to be wholly inconsistent, disparately applied, and entirely pragmatic in response to the needs of a moment. If sufficiently powerful forces and interests are unwilling to tolerate a particular operation of law at a particular time and place, it gets changed, either formally or in practice. The image of making progress toward ultimate ends is then reinforced as changes become publicized as legal "reforms" rather than as a response to the power of random forces and interests that are making themselves felt.

To make up for its lack of specific goals, the system invents apparent goals, those that seem specific. It is permeated with specifics that, on closer inspection, prove to be either ideological in nature or, actually, not goals at all, but only effects. Whatever the system does at the time is said to be its purpose. The criteria it uses to "measure" success are stated in terms of those activities it happens to be conducting and others it is equipped to do.

Take efforts at court "reform." These usually aim at enlarging the capacity of the courts to process individuals more speedily through their various existing stages. The "purpose" of the reform becomes to dispose of more cases, the means such things as the addition of judges, space, supportive personnel, and technical equipment, and the manipulation of schedules.

Presumably Justice demands speed. In one recent experiment in the administration of Justice, the following sign appeared in courtrooms and on corridor walls in the civil court of one New York City borough. It was directed TO ALL JUDGES from the court's chief judge.

Re: Conference and Assignment Parts

Cases appearing on the Conference Part calendars are for *immediate* disposition: i.e., settlement, discontinuance, dismissal or by assignment forthwith to a trial part for immediate trial subject only to the matters presently before the court.

The object is immediacy: NOW. Adjournments will not be permitted in the trial part. Where a continuance is indicated, such case must remain in the Conference Part. Good team work between the three judges [working on the batch of cases assigned to each "part"] has proved to be the key to success of this system.

In other words, digesting quantities of disputes through the system in the shortest possible time per case becomes the goal. Disgorging them out the other end of the judicial process (through settlement, discontinuance, dismissal or immediate trial) is the means.

Currently the numbers game is synonymous with Justice in this particular jurisdiction, whose watchword is NOW. But if a relatively small case backlog existed, the watchword would become DELIBERATION—as it is in places having fewer cases. Depending on the caseload, either rationalization justifies the existing system. So in this jurisdiction, "due deliberation" would simply be a code phrase for slowdown if the jurisdiction's "reform" ever eliminated its backlog. The only other adaptive alternative—judges quitting and courts being contracted—would be unthinkable.

As conditions vary, then, opposite stratagems are asserted under the same ideological banner, Justice. The actual function of both approaches is to adapt the system as may be required for its survival, to perpetuate it as closely as possible in its current form, and to enable its professionals to maintain their status largely intact. These functional goals are achieved by characterizing whatever the professional and his system are doing at any given moment as definitive of the system's proper ideology. In other words, the switches in court procedures, for example, are adaptive techniques for the purpose of warding off more fundamental change and continuing the appearance that a bureaucracy is achieving, in the words of the posted memo, "success of this system." The absence of specific goals by which court functioning can be measured makes the illusion of accomplishment possible and prevents it from being labeled—what it truly is—a flurry of self-justifying activity.

We can now return to the methods of correction.

In the same way that courts (and other law bureaucracies) justify themselves by justifying what is, a parolee's adjustment is measured by his conformity to rules that are essentially preservative of the parole organization—that are essential to its survival. The procedures with which he is required to cooperate are devised to enable the parole system to continue its operations with the fewest, farthest-between, and most superficial changes. What is meant by the universal term "successful parole" has little to do with the individual parolee's life activities and everything to do with his ability to discover and conform to what the parole bureaucracy really needs in order to conduct business as usual.

Similarly, Barry's "rehabilitation" was considered a function of the treatment center's pronouncements rather than of his actual circumstances and condition. The center's own needs and its organizational requirements determined that rehabilitation involved remaining in "the Concept" for a full "course" of "treatment"—whatever any of these words mean—prescribed for everyone entering it. Recourse to linguistic cotton-candy like "the Concept," combined with words having an authoritative scientific ring, such as "treatment" and "rehabilitation," tend to put off inquiry into what lies beneath. The layman defers to the professional and the latter has a vested interest in protecting his brotherhood. Only those who have been processed in and out, as captive customers, return to tell the story, and most are likely to end up bemused believers or to keep still in order to reap their meager rewards for having complied and "succeeded." Even if they are otherwise disposed, they are realistic enough to know that, as stigmatized individuals, their outcry is not likely to count for much in an establishment bedazzled by the Emperor's New Clothes. So long as Barry played along, monthly reports kept coming that were designed to keep him out of jail. When he left before his time was up, another report was issued—clearly reflecting the organizational wrath that had been stirred up, the sense of being rejected and even doublecrossed, and carrying the implication that there was only one place he now belonged.

Moreover, that this final report, taken together with its monthly forebears, labeled the authors as either nincompoops or liars was not enough to allay the DA's fears that jargon and gibberish would probably triumph over common sense if the case fell into the hands of a judge at that time. He himself needed more proof than what had been set before his eyes in order to consider the case "airtight." Something more than the disposition of a particular individual was at stake here. From the point of view of the rehabilitators at the treatment center, the issue was not so much that Barry couldn't easily be replaced by another youth trying to avoid a conviction. Rather, the organization's credibility, its image of professionalism, and its whole recruitment pitch was at stake. If too many users of its services walked out, either at will or when they felt ready, then the appearance of a coherent program, a system, a rationale, and of qualified workers who knew what they were doing, would be considerably impaired. Regardless of whether or not Barry was going to return to drugs, the court was being called upon to come to the aid of its party, another legal institution in distress.

The treatment center's reponse to Barry's behavior is one example of how, in the absence of any real interest in the measurement of effects, it is possible in correction (as in any other operation of the legal system) to shrug off whatever smacks of "failure" as having been caused either by the breakdown of some other part of the system or by insufficient (not irrelevant!) resources. Another illustration of this delusionary process in action is supplied by the transcript of a conference of workers on the same rehabilitation project mentioned earlier.

This time the discussants were prison educators. The speaker from whom I quote was a young woman in the counseling business. The federal Manpower Development and Training Act, which paid her salary, had decreed that it would be salutary to provide unemployed poor people with a prescribed mixture of vocational training and counseling. This fillip was now being tried out in prisons. At no loss to explain the fact that the treatment might be having little effect on the rate at which her counselees were getting into trouble once out of jail, the lady commented as follows: "I have great faith in what we are doing. And I think that what we have done is important. But I have tremendous question as to what happens to these kids when they leave this kind of setting [the prison]."

The assumption behind the young lady's comment was that the testing-ground for a program designed to prepare young inmates to function outside the prison should be nothing other than the prison itself—*before* their release. Implicitly: the evaluation of program should be left in the hands of the very people conducting it. We are reminded of what happens when other professionals—lawyers and the police, for example—are left to evaluate themselves according to their own views of what they are doing and the importance of their doing it. The lady counselor was saying, essentially, that any flops were the fault of the outside world—for which, presumably, the correctees were being prepared—and should not be considered a reflection of the correctional activities that were being carried out within the prison in the name of treatment. This line of reasoning is a natural for individuals occupationally committed to systems that function with ideological goals but without measurable standards that can be related to specific goals. The attitude is endemic to the complex of bureaucracies that make up the legal system.

One last example will suffice to illustrate the typically bemused thinking behind the representative approaches of correction. The sponsor of the correctional research project previously mentioned prepared a draft final report of its activities for the government. This sponsor, which initially received the federal moneys involved, was a psychologically oriented, "nonprofit" mental health outfit. The report's major conclusion was striking in light of the fact that, after a year's flourish of corrective and rehabilitational activity, there were, in fact, no findings of any effects whatsoever. Said the report: the jail "could be effective" if only it had the "psychological sophistication, skill and saturation of personnel necessary to produce learning." The implication was unmistakable: whatever lacks may have existed in the year's rehabilitational doings were remediable by more of the same, an increased dosage of identical activities. "Effective" the report asserted—but at what? The report was also wholly silent on the meaning of the "learning" that prisons might be expected to produce after getting their "necessary" infusion of "psychological sophistication," etc. These are fundamental questions, precisely involving specific goals. But their answers, as always, were taken for granted. The pretense was that such answers were rudimentary and self-evident. A "scientific" research report that didn't even raise basic issues, instead airily advised the law's prison component to escalate reliance on the same technique that, so far as analysis revealed, had accomplished nothing over a year's time—because these techniques were what its authors practiced. Nowhere more than in law is a system so unconcerned with learning when to apply the brakes, when the gas, and when to pull off the road for a mechanic's checkup.

9

"STREAMLINING"

When there is not enough furniture to cover all the holes in a rug, moving chairs around only exchanges one exposure for another. As our legal system gets more wear, its managers try the distraction of moving things around for as long as possible, eventually embellishing their action by shopping for additional furnishings. They instinctively frequent the same stores and there pick up old period-pieces that match what is already on hand. Because they have both a personal and an occupational stake in keeping current the only style in which they are the recognized experts, in preventing that style from suddenly dropping out of vogue, their rote conservatism is natural.

Looking, instead, for a new rug would show up the old junk for what it is and reveal the implicit managerial priority of safeguarding one's own status and preserving one's own job—by sticking with the conventional decor. Many fixtures that have been successfully palmed off as staples might then be seen as belonging in an attic and having significance only for social historians. Ideological obsessions with precedent and continuity have successfully obscured the need for a dramatic refurnishing. But these same obsessions also prevent the legal room from being kept current for its users' rational needs.

A typical rearrangement ploy is symbolized by the court wall-poster that we have already discussed. Judicial operations were to be "streamlined" by the technique of scheduling all cases for a conference. Any which the judge could not settle would be sent directly for jury selection and then, presumably, an "immediate" trial.

Only to the extent that users of the system are willing to content themselves with being distracted rather than served can this "reform" fulfill its hidden primary function of staving off a crisis greater than that which originally called it into being.

Let us examine more closely this example of the "streamlining" process.

Judges in the conference rooms of the court come under tremendous pressure to settle their assigned cases. Settlement makes their record look good. On the other hand, a judge who is not settling "enough" risks acquiring a reputation for being unable to do a task that is now publicly identified with the function, if not the essence, of judgemanship. The reasoning goes that if he is not settling cases, he is not doing his job. It is relatively easy to keep score on "job efficiency" by tabulating his overall record with reference to a performance norm derived from how many cases each day are being settled by other judges.

There is another source of pressure. The announced fate

of all cases in which the parties refuse to come to terms is immediate jury selection and trial. This fate is, in effect, a threat that is intended to make both sides amenable to compromise at the conference. Sometimes it does. Its effectiveness depends on giving no quarter to either side that might not, for a variety of reasons, actually be ready and able to conduct an immediate trial. A lawyer or client thus handicapped is counted on to reason that half a loaf is better than none. The NOW technique is also intended to call the bluff of—or dangle some reward before—those who simply have no legal leg to stand on. Unless there were many of these, settlements would be fewer and more difficult. Such cases are actually encouraged by the conference approach. In essence, the system is saying to litigants: "We'll give you one last chance. After this, the chips are down. For those of you who can't afford the whole ride, this is the last stop."

But this, too, is a bluff. And it is the judge, in the end, who is placed in the path of the backfire.

The court's jury-selection part is already clogged with cases normally sent from its regular trial-assignment part. The crisis that gave rise to the conference system in the first place was precipitated precisely because there were not enough judges, jurors, and trial rooms to process the "normal" flow of case traffic. Litigants, therefore, were waiting "too" long with their cases on the calendar before actually getting to trial. What had been perceived as an overload because of "insufficient" judges to conduct "enough" trials was sought to be remedied by actually reducing the number of trial judges—by assigning many of them to conferences. Those withdrawn from trial availability were then instructed to add cases—their conference failures—to the jury-selection part for "immediate" trial.

But if that part totally collapsed from additional strain,

the judicial image might suffer irreparable harm and reform might be exposed as just furniture shifting. This would increase the risk of radical changes that the court itself might not be able to oversee and control.

Sensing this, judges make every effort not to carry out their threat of sending cases for trial, instead becoming desperate to settle as many as possible in conference. In other words, they understand (however they get the message) that in conference each day they must pick off more cases that are on line for trial than they would handle if they were trying cases. Their actual job is to use their offices to prevent trials. (Justice is easily adapted.) Their priority is to get cases out of the judicial orbit. This can be accomplished only if they remain generally indifferent to the nature of a settlement—so long as one is reached. Meanwhile, the jury system is being preserved as currently constituted by making a trial generally inaccessible, by blocking the trial route for as many cases as possible.

Out of concern, then, for how many cases their colleagues are getting rid of and in order to keep the jury system afloat, an informal settlement-quota emerges. Just as John as a cop has to make a certain number of arrests, just as the parole officer has to elicit conformity to his bureaucracy's needs, so the judge's settlement goals become determined by his own system's requirements for survival. Like policemen and parole officers, judges, too, measure their personal success and security by their ability to achieve ends that are primarily organizational in nature. Thus they become personally identified with the essential needs of the judicial apparatus.

Whether client interests can survive the secret bargaining sessions that constitute a judicial conference is another question. The answer depends on the extent to which a lawyer is able to assert these interests against the court's urgent need to demonstrate "results." The ability to do so depends in turn on whether client and lawyer, together, constitute one integral force and interest. The reality, as we have seen, is that the lawyer in part views—and always uses—the court as an instrument for his own purposes, often *against* the interests of his client.

An experienced and persuasive judge counts on being able to identify the earliest point at which this inevitable parting-of-the-ways occurs between the interests of lawyer and client. He must exploit the breach in order to achieve his own goal of disposing of cases—of getting closure "for the record" by evicting disputes from the court system.

The lawyer's transactions at the conference illustrate his role as a triple agent—representing client, system, and self. One look into a typical courtroom marketplace will shed light on how this works.

We are in a court that has a monetary limit of $10,000. The setting is a small room set aside for conferences. It is crowded with lawyers and clients reading, talking, coming and going, or just sitting. The judge is seated behind his raised bench—or sometimes just a desk—in the front, separated from the audience by a small fence. Beyond this are allowed only lawyers whose cases are being discussed at the moment. The judge leans forward from the bench and speaks in confidential tones to the opposing lawyers standing before him, each of whom has his file at a nearby table, ready for the draw.

For openers, each lawyer presents his client's version of the facts in a few sentences. The judge makes a mental note of any weakness in either case that may become a handy pressure point later in the discussion. He then gestures the defense lawyer back a few steps, out of earshot.

"How much are you looking for counselor? Let's see your medical bills."

"Judge, this case is a piece of junk. I've got a $30 medical and can't afford to try it. Whatever you think it's worth. . . ."

"I'd take $250 and run—if I can get it for you."

"It's not *that* bad, judge. Besides, my client's some kind of nut, a domestic who thinks she's going to get rich. And she's claiming some lost earnings."

"Go talk to her and tell her she won't get rich. You've got a tough insurance company against you, with a low policy. I'll see what I can do."

With the client.

"The judge is trying to get you a coupla' hundred dollars. That's what he recommends for your case."

"*Coupla' hundred dollars!* This is a major case. I lost my memory because of the accident."

"Then how are you going to remember what happened? If you don't tell your story to the jury, the case is going to be thrown out. Besides, the doctor didn't mention memory loss, so I can't bring it up now. And he wants $300 and three days' notice to come down here and testify at a trial. I can't give him the notice, even if you can afford the money."

"I don't have $300 for him. But I've got to get at least $3,000 for the accident. This is a major case."

With the insurance lawyer.

"How much does your company have on the file?"

"Judge, we think it's a no-pay case. He can't afford to try it."

"Neither can you. He wants $750."

"He'll never get it, judge, even on a trial. Frankly, I've

got $350 to settle it. Anything else, I'd have to call the office. Of course, I've got authority for a little more, but the case doesn't warrant it. She's got just a $30 medical bill, and that looks phoney to me."

"I'm telling you to pay more. You can get socked on a trial. I'd say pay the $750."

"Impossible, judge."

"But let's see if I can get him down."

Back to the judge.

"If I can get you $450, will you take it?"

"Make it $650, judge. The woman is very difficult."

"Can't. He doesn't have near that on the file. I want you to tell her she's got to take less or lose this case. You'll get $650 on a trial, if you're lucky, after a week, and less the doctor's fee. But this time don't waste my time. Or you'll end up downstairs trying this case."

Cooling out the mark.

"I told the judge we wouldn't accept $250. He's working hard, but it's a particularly bad company. They prefer to try their cases. I told him a high figure, one you don't have a chance for. I'd say something in the neighborhood of $400 is fair. Otherwise we wait around another couple of days for a trial."

"That's impossible for me. I'm losing time from work. But $250—that's a disgrace! A friend of mine got $1,000 for practically nothing last year. These companies should lose their license."

Being reasonable.

"He's trying to talk sense to his client. But she knows you've got a considerable exposure if the case goes to the jury. It's absurd to spend this much time on this case. Your company is going to have to put an additional trial man in this court unless it starts getting realistic about settlements."

"Judge, you know I am reasonable. But this case is a piece of junk."

"I may be able to get rid of it for you for about $650."

"I'll go to $600, judge, and that's it. But see if you can save me something off that. It's my neck back at the office."

Closing the deal.

"I can get you $500."

"Judge, I finally got her to say okay at $550. I can't go back now for the $50."

"All right, you've got it. I'll make him throw in the extra."

Putting on the lid.

"I got you $550. That's more than the case is worth. You're very lucky. The guy whose car got smashed in the accident, I don't think he's getting more than $200, and he may have to have a trial. We got a good judge. He worked hard and I think this is a fair settlement, especially since you couldn't go to trial."

In this $10,000-limit court most lawyers don't expect to "ring the bell." A case whose value seems to border on that limit is ordinarily begun in a higher court, on the chance that an even larger award will be recovered. In the higher court, however, the bidding procedure is identical; the dollar figures simply refer to thousands instead of tens. The exact conversation varies in every case, depending on who holds which cards and what weaknesses there are to be exploited. The lead-offs may differ slightly. Judges' styles vary, within a severely limited range. A lawyer's reputation, personality, and the kind of case as well as its particular facts are also significant variables. Still, this conference and the particular court reform we have examined are typical, archetypes.

The question of when and for what to settle is always one involving an estimate of how much more is to be gained by hanging on. This is true, as we have seen, for the client as well as for the lawyer on *each* side. It is true in criminal cases for DA's and defense lawyers, in matrimonial cases, in negligence cases for plaintiffs' and insurance lawyers. It is true of clients, whether they are criminal defendants, accident victims, or, as with Gardofsky's landlady and neighbor, complainants and victims of an alleged crime.

The decision is reached after considering four factors: what resources—time, money, and energy—will have to be spent in order to advance a case to its next stage; how good is the offer—perhaps to plead guilty to a lesser offense, perhaps to make a money payment—compared to the likely best and worst result that may ensue, based on any number of intangibles and expectations; what alternative use can be made of the resources that would be expended if continuing the action or freed because of ending it; and what resistance will be encountered, with various others, if one opts for either continuance or a halt—for example, can the client be made to accept or comply? what will happen to the lawyer's reputation? have the newspapers pushed everyone into a corner, necessitating a knockdown, drag-out fight to the end? In weighing these factors, the lawyer, at least, is also guessing how they weigh with his opponent.

The technique of conference is old-hat, practically a definitive hallmark of the legal system. Opposing lawyers often discuss their cases over the telephone, usually before beginning the actual lawsuit. And if they have not, they often must say they have. Many courts require the lawyer to state in writing, when he is placing a case on the calendar, that "settlement has been discussed." Whatever the exchange between lawyers was intended to accomplish as an innovation and "reform," now—whether it *actually* occurs or not—it is a mere formality, one that is mechanically and automatically signified by the lawyer, who merely checks a box on a printed form.

Another official step along the route to trial is known as the "pretrial conference"—as distinguished from the separate "blockbuster" conference that we illustrated. The pretrial conference, initially hailed as the answer to congestion, is now just a stopping-off place en route to the blockbuster. (Besides these formalized conferences, intermittently during every trial, up to the moment a decision is announced, other conferences are held, sometimes in chambers with the judge as intermediary, sometimes between the lawyers only.)

The element that is really counted on to make the blockbuster conference effective as a settlement device is the illusion that it is able to convey, in part, that it is actually a last resort. All the pressures of down-to-the-wire are realistically simulated. If law is drama, then this is a play-within-a-play. The sense of urgency imparted by judges to lawyers, then by lawyers to their clients during negotiations, and, when a case is not settled, by the directive to "go downstairs immediately" (to the jury-selection part) is workable, temporarily, as a means for getting disputants to waive their "right" to have their cases decided at a trial. They become willing to pay more or to accept less—or, in counterpart criminal proceedings, to plead guilty more readily or offer greater inducements to obtaining a guilty plea—all simply to escape continued involvement in this mesh of the system that has been dropped over them—for the system's own internal, organizational purposes.

But with conference rejects gradually piling up in the jury room, the urgency fades. As its last-lap image increasingly gets recognized as a mirage, the conferencing gimmick loses its harassment capabilities and, therefore, its continued effectiveness. It gets relegated to the perfunctory role of simply another intermediate ritual—like the exchange between the lawyers before calendar, like the pretrial conference—hallowed because it exists, institutionalized along with many other rituals and remaining, for consumers, a furniture rearrangement.

10

THE TRIAL
ROUTINE

Lawyers pick juries for different reasons and with different stratagems in mind. Some arrive at the stage simply seeking to call their opponent's bluff, with no intention or hope of contacting the principals who are necessary for a trial. Perhaps their client, or a crucial witness, has died, moved, or become incommunicado. Maybe the case is an almost sure loser or simply isn't worth trying. The tactic may be to reach the trial room in the hope of having the judge there elicit an offer for the first time or get a previous offer upped. Some lawyers may even begin the trial without witnesses, and go so far as to make an opening statement to the jury. If these gambits don't pay off, either they take what they can get, or discontinue their case altogether—if they can't get anything. In a criminal trial they may suddenly switch a client's plea to guilty or else sit through the People's case, make objections and motions, then "rest." Some lawyers keep their clients "on call" —that is, available by phone—during the waiting period before trial. But many others prefer having the client in court throughout, on the theory that a long and anxiety-producing wait will make him more amenable to whatever resolution is in the offing.

Both because of these well-known variants and the court's over-riding concern for processing cases out of the system en masse, the actual trial stage isn't always what clients expect it to be. Things may appear a little hectic and, alternately, it may seem that absolutely nothing is going on. In fact, the judge in the trial part is probably juggling several cases at the same time.

He proceeds with one perhaps as far as the openings, sends the jury back to its waiting room, then huddles with the lawyers to determine whether or not these initial salvos have dislodged either side from its previous stand-pat position. The traditional technique of talking first to one lawyer and then to the next, calling each back for private consultation as the other leaves, is employed. The setting may be the courtroom, from which the jury has just been banished temporarily; it may be chambers, a hallway near the courtroom or even, in one case in which I participated, a judges' private bathroom—into and out of which "chambers" my opponent and I each walked approximately five times during the whole conference.

The longer a case promises to be, the harder the judge works at settling it. "I can't let you tie up my courtroom this long. This case has got to be disposed of now." Thus spake one judge who had sat through five minutes of a trial, recessed for conference, and heard my estimate that the whole case was going to take about ten days to present. Any

lawyer reading between the lines takes this as a signal to settle. If he doesn't cooperate and insists on a full trial, there is
always the likelihood that the judge is somehow going to use
his position to subtly influence the jury and even the score.

This estimate cannot be proven. But it has been tested
out in fairly similar circumstances. In one conference in
which I participated, for example, a judge was trying to settle a *non*jury case immediately prior to its scheduled trial
before him. This was a car accident case in which the defendant himself would be insulated from any actual financial loss. Any award would be paid by the insurance company. A group of lawyers had gotten together to form this
particular company, then hired themselves to represent its
insureds when claims were brought. The money that would
change hands was, in effect, partly the defense lawyer's
own.

In chambers the judge heard out both my own and my
opponent's claims. He considered what each side was going
to introduce into evidence, then recommended a compromise settlement, one somewhere between the "offer" and
the "demand" figures that had been mentioned. As the lawyer for the plaintiff, I accepted. But the defendant's lawyer
refused to permit "his client" to pay that amount, saying the
case wasn't "worth" it.

"All right," snapped the judge. "Try the case. Let's get it
started and over with."

After a full trial, without a jury, at which everything was
played out as both of us had outlined in chambers, the judge
rendered a verdict that was exactly twice the amount that
he himself had recommended a short while before. Presumably, the defense lawyer had to be taught a lesson. In essence, he paid a tax for using the facilities.

Leaving the attorneys to cool their heels or talk over

offers with their clients, a judge might call back a jury whose case had been suspended, for one reason or another, an hour or the day before. While jurors, clients, witnesses, and lawyers are being assembled in the case, a third jury may be rushed in, briefly, for final instructions on the law before being sent out to "deliberate." Perhaps sometime during the day, another jury's foreman signals that his panel is ready to return its verdict, and the case first before the court is recessed again while this one is wound up.

When all the preliminaries have been gotten through and a case is on for trial in dead-earnest, this situation changes. The figure of greatest importance is no longer the judge. From the lawyer's point of view, everything is now up to the jury.

The judge will exercise his influence and, if he is motivated and tries hard enough, may be able to swing the case one way or another by swaying the jury subtly. Of course, any judge who seems to want a case decided in a particular way still has to be careful about what he places "on the record." But only the *words* at a trial are taken down by the stenographer and transcribed for an appeal. So there can only be nonverbal shennanigans from the bench. Such shennanigans may consist of judicial faces and grimaces, innuendoes and tones of voice, raised eyebrows, gestures, and the like. In one case, for example, the presiding judge turned his chair aside, faced the courtroom windows and read the daily *Law Journal* throughout the entire cross examination of one of the chief witnesses.

But any trial lawyer learns neutralizing techniques for these occasions. He can often counter judicial ploys and others that are resorted to by his opponent, and may even be able to turn them to his own advantage—for example, by winning the jury's sympathy through appearing victimized, thus creating in them a championing impulse that will rebound in favor of his client. Moreover, every lawyer acquires a few gambits for his own initiative.

The point is that the professionals—lawyers as well as the judge—are now playing to the jury. Witnesses, too, have been explicitly instructed to do the same or else are coached in a way that the lawyer feels will have the maximum desired effect on jurors.

The earliest trials were spectator sports. Juries were "the rabble" and just about anyone could show up at them, at least among the propertied middle class, and have a say in the outcome. Even the more formalized and better regulated affairs were happenings of a sort: Socrates, for example, was reportedly tried by over four hundred judges. In the Middle Ages, some cases were tried, in essence, as horse shows called jousts, and the term "jousting" is still used to describe lawyers' activities in the courtroom.

Despite our switch from horsemanship to wordsmithing and the addition of a few rules governing conduct in the courtroom arena, the dominant aura in trials remains that of entertainment. Many can still come and watch, as a spectator sport. Although all but twelve are excluded from decision making in any given case, total (middle-class) community involvement—and incrimination—in the system rather than the particular case is assured because so many trials are staged.

A number of different props and trappings foster the notion of trials as dramatic entertainment. In the U.S. Supreme Court, for example, when the judges take their places at the bench, they all emerge simultaneously, on cue from the Chief Justice, from behind velvet curtains that are drawn aside. Instead of 8:40 in the evening, curtain-time is 10:00 o'clock in the morning. In the better courts of state systems, the house is filled by 10:00. In second- and third-rate (lower) courts, proceedings are often adapted to the habits of the audience, sometimes with several consecutive calendar-calls held in one morning or, to accommodate the do-it-yourself amateur, after working hours in the evening.

In line with a general movement of drama, in this country much costumery—such as powdered wigs and barristers' robes—has gone by the boards. But judges still wear their gowns, and lawyers dress to project their particular role-image to the jury. The stylized placement of furniture in a courtroom, the flag as pennant, the physical elevation of the bench in midstage—like the referee's stand in a tennis or jousting tournament—and the presence of a supporting cast, among it the witnesses and such incidental figures as the uniformed court officer who functions as usher, all reinforce this atmosphere of a theatrical production.

Normally, only artists and press critics are allowed in. Some courts are considering accomodating other media as soon as a way can be found to insure that they and their paraphernalia won't steal the show. In any event, representatives of the media are outside the stage door in larger productions, seeking interviews with and "different slants" about the starring principals—that is, reviewing the show. Hecklers, too, have their place in the gallery. With increasing frequency they are tolerated so long as the show can go on.

Consciously or not, lawyers who want to win realize that they must put on an entertainment for the jury, and whoever comes up with the most effective production does win. The practitioner's phrase, "enlisting their sympathies," is another way of saying that the jury has to be made to feel it got its money's worth. Sometimes the whole contest hinges on one of the lawyer's being able to persuade the

jury to accept his preferred characterization of the production—as drama, comedy, farce, or melodrama. In other
cases, thumbs go up or down depending on which side has
staged the better show, greater or more elaborate entertainment. Like all directors, lawyers give consideration to the
order in which the characters will make their appearance.
As the plot unfolds, there are villains and heroes, surprises,
reprises, rebuttals, and comebacks. The verdict is the ap-
plause.

The trial as entertainment cannot be precisely likened to
traditional theater. The two have common forebears but
different patterns of development. Although both seek to
blur the formal distinctions between actors and audience,
each has traditions and conventions of its own.

The client, for example, is the protagonist in that he is the
one whose fate is being decided. But he may not make an
appearance on stage and, in some cases, may not even be required in the courtroom theater at all. His role as a character in the play, nevertheless, is indispensable. Still, he usually feels like a passive spectator rather than a vital
participant. Things happen that he doesn't understand or
consider relevant. Even though it is "his" case, he often
senses that the performance is actually being conducted for
the benefit of others. It is serving the interests of the regular
repertoire troupe while he is only a pick-up actor. And to
the extent that the trial is also something of a morality play,
it serves the interests of the audience. Aside from a possible
brief appearance in the limelight, the client's role is usually
confined to that of a coach. And then he is mostly just an ad-
visor to the professionals.

The lawyer serves in his one person several functions and
plays parts that are normally filled by more than one individual. He is producer, director, maestro, script-adapter,

and, in many instances, star of the show. At the same time, he functions like a Greek chorus, "barking" the program and underscoring points that, as the plot unfolds, the jury is supposed to consider important. Still, he must share, in different degrees, all of these roles with others—the judge, client, and opposing lawyer.

Jurymen are actor-participants. But, first and foremost, they are the lawyers' audience and target. If they have prescribed roles as actors, they are, nonetheless, kept in the dark about most of the scenario until it has played itself out before their eyes. After this happens, they get the decisive role in its dénouement. Meanwhile, they have been purposely excluded from the most important cues and stage directions emanating from behind the scenes, both before and during the actual performance: the private transactions between lawyers and judge. Yet these transactions took place precisely because the jury was ready for action.

11

CHANGING
THE LAW

ALL AGENTS and agencies of the
law system have two main concerns: first procuring and
then getting rid of customers. Because people—although
not necessarily the same people—must be kept coming back
for more, both recruiting and evicting have to be done with
some delicacy. They must proceed in such a way as to preserve a constituency for the law.

In order for this continuous flow to be maintained, those
who use and support the system have to believe that what
happens while a case is enmeshed in it, somehow is necessarily and uniquely related to the end result when that case
emerges from the hopper. Most people have to accept that
a case outcome is achieved by or because of a process that
bears some relevance to whatever the law is charged with
deciding. The job of the law system, therefore, is to main-

tain an image that the methods of law actually deal, and
have a corner on the market in, some commodity or method
that is peculiarly law-ish. Intermediate legal activities have
to be accepted as bearing a logical relationship to final legal
determinations. The system cannot, for example, be seen as
another cop at the pier, primarily concerned with keeping
traffic moving—in and out. Its activities cannot be viewed
as boiling down to a frantic palming-off of cases solely for
the purpose of maintaining its existence and keeping its op-
eratives in business. What it is doing must be seen, instead,
as serving an end that is relevant to its consumers' interests
—rather than as requiring consumers to serve *its* purpose.

There would be no point, for example, in hiring a lawyer
and getting on line for trials just to give judges, lawyers,
clerks, and a host of others a place to go each day, something to do, and a regular income, partly at public expense
and partly through a toll on those who had queued up. That
uniquely law-ish something cannot be revealed as primarily
a set of organizational concerns determining results according to a random juggling of momentary priorities established
for individual self-preservation and bureaucratic self-perpetuation. If this were believed, the simplest way to relieve
the strain on the courts would be seen as abolishing them.
And once the courts were abolished, a more economic and
purposeful system for obtaining social conformity than one,
in essence, of abolishing cases that have ripened for a suitable time on a vine of rites, would soon have to be devised
—and undoubtedly would be.

The cornerstone of legal administration, then, is a general
acceptance that the existing legal happenings define Justice
and need only palliatives, trimming, ballasting, and, most of
all, additional superstructure over the same hull. This belief
is bolstered by the absence of any way to measure the ac-

tivities of the legal conglomerate against specific goals—
since there are none. And it is enhanced by the occupational
and ideological predilections of monopolistic professionals
toward maintaining precedent and continuity—or keeping
things roughly the same and making only those adjustments
that appear essential for staving off both change and collapse.

Authors receive an "advance against [sales] royalties."
Salesmen get "draws against commissions." The salaries of
police can be viewed as a kind of personal financial draw
against *ideological* commissions they are expected to earn.
The premiums they bring in are not in the form of money
but may be conceived of as public relations "brownie-
points" for the police profession. But we have seen that they
also function as recruiters for the whole, amalgamated criminal-law industry. Making arrests does more than justify having hired police in the first place. If backed up by a certain
percentage of convictions, arrests are evidence of the imperative need for more police. But besides this, arrests and convictions legitimate the status enjoyed and activities that are
performed by individuals elsewhere throughout the system.
We have illustrated this several times, as when Barry and
Gardofsky (the latter having been recruited privately, by his
neighbor-complainant) were both used as shuttlecocks—between court and treatment center in one match, between
court and observation ward in another. We have also exam-
ined the symbiotic relationship between courts, prisons, and
parole in the same light of the one justifying the other.

When someone is shoved into a paddy wagon, he is really
being pushed into a hopper that services and justifies each
of the confederated stages, processes, units, and adjuncts of
the criminal-law administration. Once ingested, he doesn't
get released until altogether digested by the administration,

that is, until each of the phases having some use for him obtains its own maximum benefits.

In fact, if the inter-relatedness of systems is seen to extend beyond the formal punishment period, we might conclude that the newly acquired social value of someone who goes through the hopper is never relinquished. Individuals with records are a customary easy mark for re-arrests, as shown by countless recidivism studies and as suggested by John's concern for maintaining credibility among his regular, steady clientele. A gigantic network of human-service operations—each with a separate set of professionals—depends for its very existence on the ability of the legal system to churn out a continuing supply of individuals who are conspicuously labeled and, therefore, are fair game to be treated as "disadvantaged."

Countless enterprises other than the legal system, both legitimate and illegitimate, rely for certain classes of their necessary manpower on the alienating and exclusionary effects of criminal stigma. For example, according to a survey conducted by the Committee on Civil Rights of the New York County Lawyers' Association and released in May 1970 ("Employment Disabilities of Former Convicts"), those in New York State who have "paid their debt to society" then find the following jobs closed to them: Veterinary, medicine, dentistry, podiatry, undertaking, embalming, real estate (brokerage and sales), notary public, insurance adjustment, billiard or bingo operating, private investigation, hospital employment (except orderlies), barbering, hairdressing, bar work. The report describes itself as preliminary and does "*not* pretend to have exhausted all such statutory and administrative exclusions." Some exclusions are mandated by law while others depend on current "policy" or a bureaucrat's discretion. Some apply across-the-board, others just to felons, while still others affect those who have been convicted of "crimes" like jostling and vagrancy. Add to this the impossibility of anyone with a record getting bonded, thus effectively knocking him out of contention for any responsible private job, plus the strong resistance of middle-class employers to taking "risks," and it is seen that those who have been recruited by the criminal-justice apparatus are likely to stay recruited for a long time. We might then agree with a young ex-convict, graduating with honors from a New York City university, who candidly announced that his career was, and would have to remain, being an ex-convict.

Police, in summary, create the business for and of all subsequent functionaries in the criminal-law conveyor-belt—defense lawyers, prosecutors, courthouse builders, judge, wardens, rehabilitators, among many others. The police protect the professionals of the legal system by insuring that there will be users for the proprietary niche maintained by each of them within the operation.

If this is true, then one way to reduce both enforcement crime and enforcement costs is to eliminate pressures at the threshold and gateway to the criminal-justice administration. These are the pressures that engender informal, unofficial arrest and conviction quotas. It might then be possible to reassess our overall allocation of resources according to specific goals.

Intensifying the recruitment stage into the hopper, on the other hand, guarantees that the number of individuals who are going to be labeled in order to satisfy a bureaucracy's need for users will also increase. One might state this relationship as a law: the level of police power determines the quantity of input to the system. A corollary is that the level of police power also determines the amount of government-

sponsored crime necessary to sustain a sufficient arrest production to justify that level—and the rationale for further
expansion to relieve consequent "strain" on all components
of the system.

Those who reason that the "fact" of increased crime—
taken for granted by newspapers and victims but hotly de-
bated by knowledgeable experts—mandates at least the response of a proportionate increase in the number of police
should consider the situation in New York City. Between
1942 and 1970, police ranks swelled from approximately
24,000 to 32,000 men. It is not surprising to find that behind
this great leap forward were statistics showing rising crime
as causing a dangerous strain on the enforcement system
and posing a major threat to society at large. Actually, however, because of trends such as disappearance of the six-day
work week, the city, along with more arrests, now has *fewer*
police man-hours at its disposal than it did in 1942, despite
its one-third total manpower increase. This indicates that
arguments about more police being required in order to prevent society from cracking up and to save the force itself
from collapse are purely subjective. Despite the predicated
crisis of "overstrain" within the police organization that was
used to justify expansion, the result of expansion was more
work—in the form of arrests—in fewer man-hours. And the
effect of this expansion on criminal doings was negligible,
or, at least, unknown, if we accept that crime has "continued" to increase. Others take the position that, to a point
at least, the proliferation of police is itself an incitement and
provocation somehow having to do with criminality. But
whether or not the per capita crime rate actually has increased, inflation of criminal activity is still being cited as a
threat to society that can be stemmed only if we adopt the
priority of more police "protection." The dynamics here are

that belief in the existence of a crisis leads to organizational escalation that is accepted as being justified if the organization merely does more of its own thing. "Crackdowns" and increased arrests validate the growth of police notwithstanding that these activities, if they don't themselves cause crime or are not themselves criminally implemented, seem unrelated to the increase that is cited by advocates of still more of the same.

The analysis that has been presented here is incomplete. Many complicating factors—such as changed technology, re-deployment of police over the decades, and demographic shifts—have not been considered because they might obscure the basic issue while, in the long-run, they would support the same conclusion.

Like the mental health outfit that recommended that government "saturate" the prisons with its kind of practice and like the lady counselor's assertion that her failures were most likely attributable to flaws not in her program but to be found somewhere else in society, police growth is simply another sign of a sort of occupational and organizational ego-centrism that boils down to every-bureaucracy-for-itself. As we have seen in all these cases, each component of the criminal-law administration feeds the other. So reinforcements on any front create an irresistible demand for more troops everywhere. This situation is underscored now and then by publications that reprint frightening newspaper accounts of social disintegration being caused by rebels, revolutionaries, vandals, hoodlums, poor people who don't know their place, and the restive young—and then reveal their sources as archives from the last century. Belief that we are at last facing the real thing impels the same tired solutions that have been tried and found wanting, in disregard of the functional consequences of expansion as the usual response to the crisis syndrome.

Police recruitment of involuntary consumers of the criminal-law administrative bureaucracy generally occurs among the lower classes. A 1969 study conducted by Herbert L. Packer, a well-known Stanford University law professor, shows that "crime in the streets"—for which most police arrests are made—victimized one out of seventy ghetto dwellers *but only one out of 10,000 among the general population!* ° No one has yet assumed that the suburbanite mugger commutes to Harlem to transact his business. The professor's figures therefore corroborate many other reports showing that the prosecution bureaucracy generally feeds on the black and the poor. For more graphic proof, one need only post himself in any criminal courtroom or check the color and appearance of inmates' relatives on the waiting line outside a city prison just before visiting hours. Most crime that arouses public concern, then, is and has traditionally been concentrated in well-known, confined locales and is committed by people living there—on their own kind. All that local citizens who are realistic can usually hope for from police stationed in the ghetto is that the latter will keep their share of the take down to a reasonable minimum and, in the process of "enforcement," cause less devastation than occurs from crime itself.

The rezoning of crime into middle-class areas stirs up a public wrath that obscures the fact that the middle class is still exposed to victimization at a rate less than one percent of that which has threatened ghetto dwellers for years without raising many hackles—and this figure does not include

° Herbert L. Packer, *The Limits of the Criminal Sanction* (Palo Alto, California: Stanford University Press, 1969.)

hidden police violence that increases the latter's risks but, by and large, does not affect the middle class. Yet it is in response to middle-class demands and needs, and along the lines of middle-class views of what solutions are required and who needs to be safeguarded, and for the assuagement, if not the benefit, of the middle class that enforcement is stepped up—in the ghetto. At the same time, the "protection" afforded by more police also involves additional forces ostentatiously placed around in bastions of the middle-class residential areas and at business centers owned and frequented by the middle class. The basic point is that suspect-hunting forays and suspicious-character roundups are conducted in the ghetto, or against blacks in neighborhoods in which they don't "belong," mostly because "extra" crimes were committed on middle-class turfs against middle-class people. It is not any questionable increase in crime that has provoked contemporary outcry so much as the fact that some ghetto dwellers have decided to expand their activities into greener pastures—for reasons that are many and complex. The consequence for the majority of law-abiding ghetto citizens is a holocaust of enforcement the likes of which had never been visited on their community for the more usual purpose of stemming indigenous crime within it.

Laws, by and large, are enacted by middle-class legislators. Civil-service jobs are held down by middle-class bureaucrats who determine the distribution of public services that are inadequate to benefit everyone equally. Power in the courts is wielded by middle-class judges and lawyers, while crucial day-to-day administration is left to middle-class "clerks" (relatively exalted positions, usually political, not to be confused with grocery-store cashiers of the same title.) Juries are composed mainly of middle-class laymen. It is mainly middle-class morality that determines how criminal Justice is applied—that is, how and to whom punishment is meted out. Correctors and their programs are as representative of the middle class as the conditions of parole are ridden with its values. If rehabilitators abandoned the pretense of taking seriously their impossible task of applying these values across-the-board, they would, perhaps, be less discouraged and cynical. But they would also be risking their organizational basis that, as we have seen, assure their middle-class jobs.

Few activities can be labeled criminal if they are in general practice among the middle class. Drugs—until recently, when they were taken up by the middle class—and "numbers" are examples of safe prosecution grist. Laws against "illegal" activities that are or have become middle-class pastimes or necessities are enforced in such a way that the middle class is insulated from all but token or nominal penalties. When the use of narcotics was mainly confined to ghettos, for example, defendants were being convicted and jailed willy-nilly for drug crimes—almost regardless of age, medical condition, the kind of drug involved, or whether they were users or pushers. Now we refer to "drug-related" crimes as having to be looked at separately, maintain a growing treatment apparatus, have kicked out of the language terms like "dope fiend," designate addicts as physically and emotionally ill and conceive of the whole situation as a "national problem"—all of which means that this "problem" has reached the middle class. To be sure, the new solutions and concepts are superior to what preceded them and benefit those from all classes—though not equally, or even proportionate to the distribution of the problem among them—but the very existence of such solutions is a reminder that we respond differently to the concerns and needs of different elements of society. Where the middle class is involved, whatever becomes widespread is likely to be functionally or officially legalized. The exercise of the law, of course, may be genteely curbed by what I have called the balance of illegality. Wherever the law opposes what is done in the middle class, it becomes effectively annulled by tacit conspiracies involving such people as Dr. Bell or the organization man setting his kickback price or the witnesses offering to lie, or by the commuters demanding openly to flaunt the rules of the road.

We have, then, a remarkable situation: a legal system maintained, at all levels, by the vital contribution of its involuntary users—and on their sufferance—yet one that is structurally dedicated to perpetuating the individual and class interests of those who manage and control it.

This situation can continue only so long as these involuntary users remain conned by an ideology that persuades them to accept fiction as reality. They must believe that their interests get satisfactory representation in the system, that they are more than grist for the bureaucratic mill that is processing them. Otherwise, as is beginning to occur, they will simply refuse to be tried.

¶ POLITICAL PROTEST TRIALS

This is really the crux of so-called political protest trials: the defendants disown the law's jurisdiction over them.

It is true that these trials drum up free publicity for causes that might not otherwise get featured in the media.

But traditional—that is, favorable—"public relations" for defendants cannot be considered more than a fringe benefit of a political trial. Such publicity requires an intelligent exposition and sympathetic presentation, in terms that the general public can understand. Most defendants feel they will never get coverage of this quality at the hands of a press they genuinely consider hostile, controlled, and, *perhaps,* uncomprehending. They are after something different. Any notion that their often grotesque and provocative courtroom antics are carried on in the expectation of favorable coverage would imply a considerable faith in "establishment" institutions. But, in fact, a complete absence of faith underlies their tactics, which are built, instead, on a cynically functional analysis of how courts and the press do react and interact, not on how things are "supposed" to work.

Still, it is obvious that defendants who opt for political trials are courting a certain kind of publicity and seeking to manipulate the communications media. Usually they are "on stage" from the moment their cases reach the limelight. These performances, both in and out of the courtroom, are somehow intended to further their political and ideological goals, if not their legal interests.

The antic behavior of political defendants seems an attempt to reach through and beyond the institutions of press and trial. The defendants are trying to contact the general public directly, using the "captive" press solely for a mechanical purpose, transmission, but not accepting any of its usual interpretative functions as valid or legitimate. Hi-fi engineers design and redesign their equipment to be acoustically invisible. Their aim is to perfect the transmission of "original" sounds without interference. In the same way, these defendants are seeking a means to reach a mass audience, perhaps an imaginary one, without their particular message becoming distorted in the transmission process. They, too, want the original content left intact, including its political nuances and shadings of tone and color.

The subject of their intended communication is law, how it operates, whom it serves and protects, and why it is after such people as themselves. Inferentially, too, in the means they adopt for conveying their message as well as in its substance, they are commenting on all of the major institutions of government and modern society. For example, in resisting the traditional usage of the press and relying, instead, on many-dimensional, virtually encoded transmissions—including dress, decorum, gestures; in short, on the startling and the unexpected—they are calling attention to the fact that the kind of reportage and description that we are accustomed to accept as complete is, indeed, shallow and partial in relaying even the nub of an event.

A political trial may be truly illustrative of the medium being the message. Only at first glance is it ironic that, to achieve their desired clarity, defendants frequently avoid forthright verbal statement and try to come across, instead, by means of both *symbolic* and *demonstrative* communication. Their language is often obscure, seemingly imprecise and loaded with tantalizing double meanings. Much more of substance seems to be implied in their garish, faintly appealing life styles, in the uncompromising energy of their resistance to we-know-not-quite-what, their ponderous, and seemingly profitless, drawn-out legal maneuvers, their exaggerated and restless political posturings, and their vulgarity, so clearly designed only to provoke and for the shock value of pointing up hypocrisy in many of our social conventions.

There are good likely reasons for their not simply stating

outright what is to be said. Many defendants reject aspects of a society that they consider pseudo rationalistic. Their intention is to demonstrate that "proper" language is, itself, politically and culturally tainted. That is, normal verbal communication presumes and imposes a commitment to traditional thinking and is therefore not an appropriate vehicle for communicating radical ideas of any sort. The old linguistic conventions seem shop-worn, inadequate for imparting the urgency of making certain important changes immediately and of tapping many levels of understanding between people now. These conventions seem intrinsically to foreclose the possibility of communicating on levels other than those which are formal and superficial.

If Joyce made literary English stereophonic, these defendants, then, are at least pointing to the possibility of legalese becoming four-channel and omni-directional. They force its users to hear "new" sounds, to adapt and react to stimuli outside the scope of what is considered the normal and proper declaratory mode. They intend to demonstrate that both this norm and the idea of its propriety are themselves outmoded—because they close minds. Those language forms that the law rules "relevant," "admissible," and "material" seem insufficiently rich and connotative to be the screening-out grid for what gets "on the record." The law, so the reasoning goes, must be made to take account of more than an immediate act or a specific situation in making its judgments. The system must become responsive to a context that includes a consideration of how the law is enforced, how all segments of the population are living, and what they—and not only the middle class—actually have to do in order to get what they need and want.

In putting other groups on a par with the middle class, their reasoning continues, the system is going to have to become less preoccupied with saving its own skin through the device of "making a record." Although this device may be useful for fulfilling the formal and ritualistic requirements of the law, it simply makes no sense in terms of the human situation that is often before the court. The defendants dramatically make this point by putting themselves in the role of victims and scapegoats. Hurling essentially insignificant barbs and insults at the system, they aim to provoke retaliation that is obviously harsh and extreme. This creates a sort of animated political cartoon, which reveals the law engaged in the repressive and stamping-out behavior that they claim is typical but that is normally camouflaged.

Another of their demonstrative tacks is to respond in open court with jargon, profanity, and slang that is unprecedented in that setting. By this means they, in effect, demonstrate how inadequate and beside the point the refined logic of the law seems to them. This verbal behavior is one way of signaling that legal logic does not take into account much that is appropriate and relevant in transactions that are made in the hurly-burly of street life and urban conditions.

Once again, bizarre behavior is a useful way of calling attention to the overall problem of noncommunication within the society. The gravity of this problem is contrasted with the inadequacy of the means that have been designed to cope with it—the official institutions of communication—at least as currently managed. The media are implicitly shown up as purveyors of levity. The entertainment of a staged and superficially vacuous courtroom "happening" gets full and faithful coverage. But a message of straightforward political and social dissent, coming from the same source, could not get by without being garbled in transmission or editorially emasculated. If the defendants' message embedded in these happenings actually gets through to the intended audience, they feel they have achieved the same success as guerrillas who outfit themselves with captured supplies and who fight the enemy with weapons of its own manufacture.

Assuming these general political purposes, what, specifically, are protesters trying to demonstrate *to* the legal system at their trials? It might seem foolhardy, for reasons just stated, to attempt any summary in purely verbal form. Nevertheless, the conceptualized manifesto that follows is intended to sketch in why the tactics that are invariably adopted are disruptive and seem irrelevant—*by traditional standards*—to issues that are supposed to be resolved at a trial.

What they are "saying" goes something like this:

> You can force us into court. But not to accept your basic premise: that what's supposed to be going on here is legitimate.
>
> Why shouldn't we be disruptive? This is the best way to provoke a reaction that illustrates the thinness of the system's veneer, its basic intolerance. Besides, being disruptive is the only course that you leave open. Our other choice is to surrender before we begin, because you insist on focusing on one narrow, technical issue: legal guilt or innocence. We're really having a scrap about what is to be put upon the agenda. Your concern is far from our own. We feel that questions of "did-he-or-didn't-he" cannot fairly be taken up while real power within the legal and social structure is not within our grasp. You must be made to see how the legal system perpetuates this inaccessibility—by its labeling process, by forcing certain people and classes into practically a life's work of jousting with the law in a side arena. While they are thus preoccupied, performing the service of keeping your law operatives in status and business, the main action goes on in center ring elsewhere.

We won't be delayed with your tinkering promises of symbols of reform—since you're not delaying the prosecution. So long as it continues, we feel entitled to try the triers, the law itself, its judges and the lawmakers—and to reveal the real beneficiaries of their "due" process. You, not we, asked for this trial. Having now been brought to bay, we claim that your definition of what's relevant in this setting is simply not relevant for us, that it's just a smokescreen. Traditional courtroom protocol and decorum are for those who accept the rules at face value, who are willing to play against the house. If our claims are out of order at the trial, where else should they be raised—when, in effect, we're being tried for attempting to raise them elsewhere?

In addition, the very claim we are asserting depends on your being able to understand the *emotional* content of what we have to say. We're not involved in a game of chess but a blood-and-guts battle for survival—not only our own but that of a very important experiment in civilization, one that we're trying to preserve. As combatants, we're very serious, and totally involved.

It is, then, *your* system that gives *us* no choice. The legal rules that we stretch taut to their limits are the ones of your making, not those we would select. If we haggle, harangue, and seize upon every technicality, we're only pointing up that the system could not work if everyone were informed and demanded what you say he's entitled to. If we don't "cop out" and compromise but, instead, take the long route of making you prove what you claim, we are only making clear the tremendous costs you would have to pay if everyone else did the same. You might more fruitfully apply these costs to an investment in changes of a substantial sort. If we tweak the dignity of judges and expose their posturing as superficial, we are only saying that the trappings of dignity cannot dignify a system that doesn't perform, for us, when it is being leveled against us. Dignity is appropriate, but not when it's a mask. If we disturb the prescribed decorum of a courtroom, it is because that decorum is misleading. It is the token you accept as proof that the law is functioning properly.

We demand that you move over and make room for our interests—on terms that are meaningful to our realities. If you don't, then at least we'll make you give up the pretense that law is anything but a Wizard-of-Oz system.

Whether or not we win has to do with the ultimate inflationary costs of resisting change. You may be willing to divert unlimited resources into enforcement, prosecution, and punishment, or to sacrifice the rights of many just to be able to hunt us down. Or maybe you'll manage to live with a law that operates, even more blatantly than at present, on the double standard, permitting business as usual for its middle-class users and, at the same time, stepping up the business end of its activities against those who dissent. But these are only stopgaps. Sooner or later you are bound to run up against a revolt. The costs spiral endlessly, the overall economics are extremely inefficient, the ultimate yield self-defeating. In order to accelerate this realization, outnumbered as we are, we must have recourse to scare tactics. We are fighting illusion with illusion, using flair, seizing the stage and grabbing the "mike" at every opportunity, making the big noise. The play's the thing to convince you that an accommodation better be reached soon. Our next production might be scarier still—and more costly.

A political defense depends upon defendants being able to manipulate the rules of law as they are, something that requires the skill of sympathetic legal technicians. Small wonder, then, that the defendants are recognized, accurately, as being contemptuous of the court and its processes. But their lawyers—especially to other members of the profession—are generally regarded as traitors. They become outcasts in the trade—for having betrayed professional secrets, exploited the weak points of the system, and flouted the official pillars and shibboleths of the very structure that provides them, and so many others, with livelihood and a special standing. Sampson, too, with his long hair, brought down the pillars of the temple—upon himself, as well as all the priests. It is in keeping with an expected sense of danger among members of the bar that the American College of Trial Lawyers, the nation's leading organization of courtroom lawyers, recently issued a report calling on judges to ban from the courts, for as long as six months, any lawyer who "willfully contributes to disorder in the courtroom." The report recommended that lawyers who participate in "aberrations" of courtroom conduct should be cited for contempt immediately, as soon as they act up, without the benefit of a trial. Said the document: "control is needed. . . ."

¶ LAW AT THE SCRIMMAGE

For all that legal "principles," tranquilizers for the conscience of the winners, are able to justify any state of affairs, the law nonetheless does deal with what actually happens to people. Thus, it is always changing, because there is a limit to what some people will put up with in order to resist change and what others will tolerate just because things have always been done that way. In this sense, law rests on the consent of those who make themselves felt.

Recently, every day over about a week's time, I watched lower Broadway, in New York, being taken over, alternately, by helmeted construction workers and college students.

When the ominous murmur got so loud that I could hear it all the way up on the seventeenth floor, from my far end of the building, I knew it was about lunchtime. Outside, there was a weird feeling in the air, one of festivity mixed with a sort of hysteria that brooked no dissent. Usually, confetti was flying down from the skyscraper walls of Broadway—no matter whose turn it was to be stampeding in review. Sometimes, two masses congregated simultaneously —separated by only a couple of ranks of blue-helmeted Tactical Patrol Force police—New York's riot cops.

For some, a particularly big rally was a bonanza. On days when demonstrations were publicized, the hotdog men hurried down Broadway to get positioned early, before the sidewalks got mobbed and police barriers positioned. Their carts were provisioned to the hilt as they headed for safe spots near the center of the action, hoping to get sold out soon and go home.

Lawyers rarely join a march. In private conversations, they generally sympathize with those carrying flags. With their secretaries and colleagues, they watch from the lobbies and windows, discuss, opine and wait, inevitably to reap the harvest and get called upon. Like the hotdog men, they stand ready to treat with all sides, selling from their own cart of arguments. Mostly, their commitment is only to hiring out their wares: words spoken in noisy or subdued, airless chambers, logically forged, written after the fact, shaping the fact.

The therapeutic effect of doing one's own thing is substantial. Police ring the field, the people divide up sides—about evenly—and scrimmage savagely against each other. Then they go home. On other days, I watch concerned people sign their names to a piece of paper and then walk away convinced that their act bore some relationship, say, to controlling pollution—just because certain words headed the petition. Meanwhile, skies grow thicker.

What is happening now in the country has already been described, in another retrospect:

> America . . . constantly swept by epidemics of movements which ebbed and flowed, merged and split apart, as men and women earnestly sought the most effective means to reform society. The intellectual ferment of the times at work in a . . . country that was culturally isolated to a great extent from the rest of the world expressed itself in curious ways. Any cause whose appeal was either humanitarian, pseudo-scientific or religious, or which promised freedom from old beliefs and restraints, found enthusiastic followers.[*]

The author was writing in 1938 and describing the nation during the 1850's.

Because it is just another arena for battles that occur on Broadways throughout the land and in the minds and emotions of combatants, law cannot answer the questions that are haunting our country. It provides some with a way to

---

[*] Joan London, *Jack London and His Times—An Unconventional Biography* (New York: The Book League of America, 1939).

make living with a problem seem tolerable. This it does not by offering solutions but by consuming energies—until solutions that are temporarily acceptable have been hammered out. Like a referee, it proclaims winners—but after the fight. It is only one, and a fairly rigid and ineffectual, means for putting an official, seldom an actual, end to disputes. In and of itself, it has no values. Its morality stems from the people in charge, those who run, use, and tolerate the system for their own ends and as representatives of particular forces and interests.

A first step necessary to redistribute the balance between these forces and interests has already taken place: new people are on the streets. They should be. After all, it is not those with the all-year-round summer homes who are going to choke on the air first. The next step is to realize that turning out on the streets or turning on in the courtroom is not an end-all, but only symbolic action—with limited potential. New ideas, and an appreciation of the urgency of trying them out, are required. Lunch-hour marches, fists, feet, and slogans randomly affect—but do not necessarily improve—courts, schools, politics or the economy. So there must come a time when we deal with solutions directly, and not with symbols, when we come together for a purpose other than to scrimmage ourselves senseless as the problems multiply.

With respect to the operation of the legal system, the Middle Class Burden of enforcing legality one way among the controllers and another among the have-nots is not going to be laid aside lightly. Those who wield the power have too vital a stake in the system to want real change. And they must have someone to wield it over. And those to whom it offers solace either do not comprehend the enormity of various costs that will have to be expended in order to implement change or, if they do, seem unprepared to meet these costs. Surely there are perfectly understandable reasons for their entrenched attitudes. But it is unrealistic to expect any congenial coming-together in this country, under its existing legal system, unless and until class integration and assimilation has taken place within the centers of social control, a process that should start with all the associated bureaucracies and institutions of the law.

Recently, I heard a judge yelling at a defendant to shut up, speak only when spoken to, and then only through his lawyer. Considering this spectacle of uneven confrontation between two classes, two distinct levels of power, and in this instance two races, I thought of a phrase sometimes used by high school drug users when they have been lectured about the evils of taking drugs. "Don't talk the talk," they say, "unless you've walked the walk."

¶ WALKING THE WALK

We, the inmates of the ninth floor of Tombs City Prison, Manhattan, N. Y., submit this petition of grievances and we solicit your attention in this matter.

GRIEVANCES

1. We address ourselves to what we feel to be the injustices we suffer in the courtrooms of the Criminal Court and the Supreme Court of Manhattan County;

(a) Many of us have been denied preliminary hearings in Criminal Court;

(b) Those of us who do receive hearings are usually given sham hearings that border on a system of Kangaroo Courts in which we are not given a chance to take the stand in our own behalf, nor are we ever advised of our rights by the judges of these so-called hearings;

(c) Many of us find ourselves the victims of excessive bails;

(d) Many of us are brought to court and wind up sitting in the detention cells all day and never get to enter the courtroom (This is generally regarded as a move by the people's representative, the district attorney, to wear the man down so that he will be willing to plead guilty):

(e) Many of us have submitted writs and petitions to the court asking that the court rectify some error in procedure. We are denied hearings on our writs even though constitutional questions are involved, or, as is usually the case, the writs go unanswered;

(f) Many of us have been waiting for trial dates for an average of eight months to a year or more and our motions for speedy trials are ignored by the courts.

In conclusion of grievance No. 1, it appears that each and every one of us has been denied some basic constitutional right and we stand before the public at large guilty until we can prove ourselves innocent.

2. In relation to grievance No. 1, in most instances we find that the Legal Aid Society aids and abets the incursions and abuses of our rights in the courtrooms. It is the order of the day for the assigned legal aid, on first meeting his client to open the conversation by saying "I suggest that you take a guilty plea," or "I can speak to the District Attorney and get you (this or that) plea."

All this without even asking the client in confidence whether he is in fact guilty of the charge. Those of us who have to rely on the Legal Aid Society to represent us find that though they are paid by the state they will not thoroughly investigate the case or subpoena witnesses in our behalf.

In conclusion of grievence No. 2, we feel that under the present system of the courts that we cannot receive any justice and can only suffer threat, coercion and intimidation disguised as law and justice.

3. We now address ourselves to the physical brutality perpetrated by the officials of Tombs Prison against the inmates thereof. This unnecessary brutality has been largely directed against the black and Puerto Rican inmate population. We vehemently denounce this policy of inhumane treatment.

It is common practice for an inmate to be singled out by some Correction Department employe because he did not hear the officer call his name or because the officer did not like the way this or that inmate looked or because of the manner in which the inmate walked or because the officer brings the turmoil of his own personal problems to work with him, and together with other officers, beat the defenseless inmate into unconsciousness, often injuring him for life physically and mentally or both.

The attacks on the inmates are made by officers wielding blackjack, night sticks, fists and feet. After such attacks it is the policy of the officials in collusion with any one of the institution doctors to fix up fake accident reports to cover up the mayhem that has been committed against the person of the inmate.

We reject all official denials that such things do not happen here as there are those of us who have experienced these sadistic attacks and there are witnesses to verify the fact. It is common knowledge by thoughtful men that "Not one leaf of a tree could turn yellow without the silent knowledge and consent of the tree itself."

That is in relation to the officers who daily brutalize and maim us. These acts would not and could not happen without the knowledge and consent of the Commissioner of Correction, the Assistant Commissioner of Correction, the Warden of Tombs Prison, the Deputy Wardens of Tombs Prison, and the Captains of Tombs Prison.

In conclusion of grievence No. 3, We DEMAND that this policy of physical brutality cease immediately.

4. In relation to grievance No. 3, it has come to our attention that our wives, sisters and mothers have been variously insulted and indecently proposed to by the officers of Tombs Prison when they come to visit us. We demand that this abuse to our women be discontinued.

5. We now address ourselves to the food which we are fed. Molded bread; only enough jelly to put on one slice of bread; rotten potatoes, always half-cooked; powdered eggs with the consistency of overcooked tapioca; not enough desserts; the food is generally unpalatable without seasoning and not fit for human consumption. In conclusion to this grievance we demand better prepared food.

6. Because many of us feel that we cannot get a fair shake between the Legal Aid Society and the courts, we find that we must prepare our own briefs and motions. This institution has law books in its library, but the institution does not allow the inmates to use the law book for reference data. In conclusion of grievance No. 6 we demand use of the law books in the library.

7. This entire institution is ridden with body lice, roaches, rats and mice and we demand that adequate measures be taken to alleviate this condition.

8. As has been stated, a great majority of the men here spend about an average of eight months to a year here with their cases and a good portion of them, due to circumstances, have no other clothes to wear save those which they had when they entered the institution. We feel that the institution should supply each inmate with adequate clothing and facilities to maintain the upkeep of their civilian attire.

9. We ask that there be an improvement in the medical staff here at the institution. As the matter now stands, the doctors prescribe an assortment of pills for every individual ailment without adequate diagnosis of the patients' com-

plaint. The doctors even relegate responsibility by having an institution nurse listen to prisoners complain of ailments and prescribe pills for that ailment contrary to standard medical practice and the law in that regard.

10. We ask that there be no repercussions against any of the inmates involved in this protest, and that each and every point of the above list of grievances be given your personal attention. We also ask that this entire petition, without deletion, be made public by giving access to it to the press.

IN CONCLUSION

We are firm in our resolve and we demand, as human beings the dignity and justice that is due to us by right of our birth. We do not know how the present system of brutality and dehumanization and injustice has been allowed to be perpetuated in this day of enlightenment, but we are the living proof of its existence and we cannot allow it to continue.

The manner in which we chose to express our grievances is admittedly dramatic, but it is not as dramatic and shocking as the conditions under which society has forced us to live. We are indignant and so, too, should the people of society be indignant.

The taxpayer, who, just happens to be our mothers, fathers, sisters, brothers, sons and daughters should be made aware of how their tax dollars are being spent to deny their sons, brothers, fathers, and uncles justice, equality, and dignity.

Respectfully submitted
WE ARE ONE PEOPLE
THE INMATES OF THE
9TH FLOOR TOMBS PRISON°

° Text of the demands issued by prisoners at the Manhattan House of Detention for Men as reprinted by the *New York Times*, August 11, 1970.